YOUR WORD IS YOUR BOND

YOUR WORD IS YOUR BOND

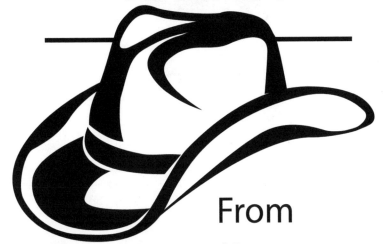

From
Rex W. Tillerson

LESSONS IN LEADERSHIP

By Perry L. Cochell

www.scouting.org

ISBN 978-0-692-90664-4
Jacket design by Jesse Stark
Printed and bound in the United States of America

Contents

"Always bear in mind that your own resolution to succeed
is more important than any other thing."

Abraham Lincoln

Foreword

On January 19, 1961, a strong nor'easter slammed into Washington, D.C., blanketing the city under 8 inches of snow and ice. Despite the massive storm, the U.S. Army Corps of Engineers was directed to do whatever it took to clear the streets so that the inauguration of John F. Kennedy as the 35th president of the United States could take place outdoors on the steps of the U.S. Capitol the next morning.

The Commander of the Engineers quickly discovered that even with several hundred troops backed up by 1,000 District of Columbia workers using plows, sanders, and even flamethrowers, clearing the snow in time for the ceremony might just be impossible. Of course, not getting the job done was not an option. The Commander picked up his phone at 2:00 a.m on inauguration morning and placed a call to the one organization he knew could deliver the assistance he needed to complete the mission: the Boy Scouts of America.

By the time the snow flurries subsided and the sun rose above the Capitol dome on inauguration morning, nearly 1,700 Boy Scouts and their leaders were fanned out along the city streets leading to the east portico of the U.S. Capitol. They shoveled out hundreds of stranded cars, cleared the main roads of snow, and scraped snow and ice off of pedestrian sidewalks. The Scouts finished their task in time for many of them to see the new president take the oath of office under a cold, sunny sky just before 1 p.m.[1]

The president later thanked a delegation of D.C.-area Scouts for their help when they visited the White House.

What made that occasion even more memorable was the fact that John F. Kennedy was the first American president in history who had been a Boy Scout.

The values of leadership that Scouting promotes were deeply ingrained in Scouting culture long before President Kennedy took office, of course. Since the day it was founded in 1910, the task of instilling the principles and practice of leadership into every new Scout has been a top priority of the organization.

You don't have to look far to see the results of that enduring focus. In the field of governance, for example, Scouting has a long and distinguished history of helping to equip local, state, and national leaders with the tools, skills, and attitudes to effectively represent their constituents. Among the 535 members of the 113th Congress (which met through January of 2015), 192 participated in Scouting. That's more than a third of the entire United States Congress! Add to that list 18 currently serving state governors and three sitting members of the U.S. Supreme Court, and it is clear that Scouting's continuing role in the development of outstanding leaders is deeply embedded in the fabric of American life.[2]

American business leaders also have deep historical ties to Scouting. Stephen D. Bechtel Jr., namesake and pioneer benefactor of the BSA's Summit Bechtel Family National Scout Reserve, was at the helm of one of the world's leading construction and engineering firms for over three decades. Mr. Bechtel is an Eagle Scout. In the field of exploration, Neil Armstrong, the first human to set foot on the moon, also attained the rank of Eagle Scout. And, Gerald R. Ford, 38th president of the United States, was the first Eagle Scout to ascend to that office. In short, to look through any directory of distinguished leaders in American science, technology, media, the arts, industry, education, governance, and business is to come across Scout after Scout after Scout.

Each of these leaders—no matter what kind of work they went on to do—shares one thing in common: a formative Scouting experience that was instrumental in shaping the paths they took in the future. Many of them tell me stories about the leadership skills they first learned, practiced, and sharpened in their respective troops. Planning meals, assigning camp chores, encouraging younger troop members, knowing when to push and when to pull—responsibility by responsibility, leadership decision by leadership decision—Scouting helped prepare these future leaders to be forward-thinking, decisive, thoughtful, and fair.

These are among the core attributes of leadership that thousands of American leaders became familiar with through Scouting. Those fundamental skill sets were enhanced, broadened, and deepened by study at college, during service in the military, on the playing field, and for many, through long years of apprenticeship in private-sector business or as self-employed owners of their own enterprises. It is gratifying to hear how many accomplished leaders look back on their Scouting experience as the place where the seeds of their lifelong appreciation for leadership were first planted and nurtured.

The Boy Scouts of America is justifiably proud of the leadership roles that have been played by Scouts in the past century across all sectors of American life. That pride is matched by an acute awareness of the paramount importance of the mission to train current and future generations of leaders, Scout by Scout. An important part of that ongoing mission is the book you are holding in your hand.

We in Scouting have long appreciated that there was a vast and diverse treasure trove of accumulated wisdom, experience, motivational stories, and life lessons store-housed by former Scouts who had reached the pinnacle of influence within their chosen fields. That very significant fact raised an equally important question: How could that enormously large reservoir of invaluable insight, practical information, and real-world experience about leadership be tapped, distilled, distributed, and utilized for the benefit of

Scouts today, and for generations to come?

That question has been foremost in my mind for a long time. In my role as director of the Office of Philanthropy for the Boy Scouts of America, I have been privileged to meet many of the nation's most outstanding leaders. Each has excelled in his or her chosen field. From aviation and engineering to logistics and natural resources development, from hotel and restaurant operations to construction, real estate, and technology, I have been fortunate to meet former Scouts from just about every kind of business one can identify on the global map. Over time I observed that as much as these individuals might differ in their adult backgrounds and experiences, there are two things they share in common: First, they are deeply appreciative for the training they received in their youth as Scouts. Second, they strongly desire to pass the lessons they learned in Scouting—and in life—to following generations.

In the summer of 2016, we took an important step toward achieving the objective of helping leaders share those lessons with the Scouting community when ground was broken for the leadership complex at the Summit Bechtel Reserve.

At this historic event, the Boy Scouts of America honored the namesake and founders of this premier youth leadership venue. The namesake, Thomas S. Monson, has given a lifetime of extraordinary service to the Scouting nationally and throughout the world. He has received both the BSA's and World Scouting's highest awards of Silver Buffalo and Bronze Wolf, respectively, and is the longest-tenured member of the National Executive Board in BSA history. The four founders of the Thomas S. Monson Leadership Excellence Complex, John D. Tickle, Rex W. Tillerson, J. W. Marriott Jr., and Philip M. Condit, each have moving testimonies about how Scouting impacted their lives in a profound way, inspiring them to provide transformational leadership opportunities for young people. All of them have set themselves apart as leaders within their professions, and each is one of the very rare individuals to be bestowed with both the Distinguished Eagle Scout Award and Silver Buffalo Award for his exceptional service on behalf of youth.

The leadership complex comprises three primary venues. The John D. Tickle National Training and Leadership Center will provide essential training to ensure that Scouts and adult leaders at every level of Scouting have the tools they need to provide the highest quality Scouting programs available. Scott Summit Center will feature the Rex W. Tillerson Leadership Center, which will offer various leadership modules in half-day experiences where Scouts participating in any Summit Bechtel Reserve program, from the Paul R. Christen National High Adventure Base to the national Scout jamboree, can spend a portion of their time learning invaluable leadership skills through experiential learning. On Leadership Ridge, the J.W. Marriott, Jr. Leadership Center will offer extended multiple-day leadership training and experiences in a more contemplative environment. It will be supported by Philip M. Condit Pointe as a primary venue for participants to reflect on their leadership journey and challenge themselves to achieve their potential.

Among the core offerings at the complex will be an ever-growing series of monographs that focus on the topic of leadership. Each monograph is based upon interviews with a former Scout who has gone on to achieve leadership positions of national and international prominence in his or her career, and who has also provided support and expertise for Scouting initiatives, including the Summit Bechtel Reserve. Each new book in the series will take its place in the complex's libraries to encourage the promotion of youth leadership and character development.

The books will be as wide-ranging as the topic of leadership itself. Each relates the path taken by one individual that brought him or her to a place where the consistent application of sound and ethical leadership principles were often all that stood between success and failure for the business or organization. These are not books on leadership theory; they share real stories about real events that brought into sharp focus both the short-term and long-term consequences of decisions made by leaders on the front lines. Readers of all backgrounds—especially youth—will have the opportunity to get to know the subjects of these books as real people who remained true to their principles through good times and bad. The leaders profiled are not hoisted up on pedestals. Instead, they are introduced as if they were standing behind a lectern in a small group classroom, eye-to-eye with their students, be they Scouts, Scout leaders, or the public at large.

Leadership is an art, based in science. It can be modeled, and it can be both taught and learned. Those who argue that leaders are born, not made, are only partly right: I believe that every person who is provided the opportunity to do so can benefit from instruction in leadership skills. To the extent that includes nearly every person everywhere, it is fair to say that leaders are born.

However, to become an effective, efficient, encouraging leader who sets the right tone in the never-ending quest to do the right thing for his business, community, or organization, the leader must first be a student. Some of that education will be delivered by life experiences. Some will come by accident. And some will come through stories, study, and reflection as found in the *Lessons in Leadership* series.

Wherever you may be reading this book, I wish you well on your own journey to acquiring and utilizing the kinds of leadership skills that each of the subjects in this series has so superbly demonstrated. If you are fortunate enough to visit the Summit Bechtel Reserve in person (including a visit to the Thomas S. Monson Leadership Excellence Complex), take a moment to stand outside on the high ground and look out over the facility. Everything that you see, every building and adventure base feature, every trail and tent and bike and zip line, every education center and every event taking place at the amphitheater is there because individuals who love Scouting applied the leadership principles they acquired over a lifetime to make everything you are looking at become a reality.

Now, it is up to you to take on your own mantle of leadership and share the fruits of the wisdom and experience you gain over the years with your generation and the generations that follow. That is the essence of leadership.

On behalf of Scouts and Scouting supporters everywhere, I want to thank each of those who are profiled in these books for their extraordinary generosity, for the commitment of time they made to the process of writing the books, and, especially, for their demonstration of leadership qualities that have distinguished their careers and their lives. Generations of Scouts will forever be in their debt.

Perry L. Cochell
Irving, Texas

[1]Samenow, Jason (2009, January 5) Inauguration Weather: The Case of Kennedy. *The Washington Post*

[2]www.scouting.org/About/FactSheets/Congress.aspx

"Talk low, talk slow, and don't talk too much."

John Wayne

Prologue

October 1878

Arizona Territory

THE RANCHER AND HIS SON SWUNG THEIR HORSES off the rock-strewn mountain trail and trotted over to the rim of the slope that swept down the mountain to the green valley floor a mile below. It was late afternoon, and the warm yellow sun was beginning its descent behind the granite range they had been climbing the better part of the day.

The weather had been unseasonably hot for October, but when they made camp in an hour or so they would need to break out their heavy jackets and lay their bedrolls close to the fire.

Father and son were quiet for a moment as they looked out over the expanse of their ranch. The main house and outbuildings looked like playhouses from this height and distance. Smoke curled into the sky from the kitchen chimney, a sure sign that the rest of the family would be sitting down to eat something a bit more hearty than the beans, bacon, and sourdough bread they would be sharing in a while.

A cool wind carried the faint lowing of cattle up the mountainside. The rancher methodically counted the cows that were spread out along the banks of the creek. Several were just visible under the branches of the cottonwood trees that dotted the creek. Any time now his oldest son and the hired hand would ride out and begin to herd them all back into the fenced corral they had hastily built when the attacks started a few nights ago.

As he thought about the attacks the rancher's hand slid down to the rifle scabbard holding his .50 caliber Sharps. He glanced over at his 14-year-old son and was pleased to see the boy was checking the strap on his own Winchester '76. Somewhere up here among the scrub pine and rocks was the mountain lion that had killed three of his calves. He didn't normally like calving in the fall, but a number of his spring calves had died from scours, and he could not afford to lose any more—not with the bank payment coming due.

"You doing all right son?" the rancher asked. He wasn't concerned about how the boy would do with the ride up the mountain or camping out for as long as it took them to find that big cat. They had hunted deer in the hills since his son was 7 or 8; he was already an experienced shot, a good tracker, and he knew how to take proper care of his horse and his gear. Life on a ranch in the middle of nowhere taught a young man responsibility at an early age.

No, it wasn't being up here that the rancher thought might be of concern to his son. It was why they were up here. When tracking a mountain lion the role of who is prey and who is predator can get confusing. The rancher had gotten close to one during a hunt. From behind a tree he was able to see the small black flecks in the lion's golden-green eyes just before it sprang on a whitetail deer. The cat sunk its fangs deep, and then, as easy as if it was carrying a rag doll in its mouth, it leapt over a 6-foot-high thorn bush and loped into the shadows with its meal.

The boy pulled lightly on his bridle, and walked his horse back a few steps from the rocky ledge.

"About the cat?" he said. He tipped his hat back, something his father knew he only did when he had something serious on his mind.

"No, I expect I'm not really bothered about it," he finally said. "It's gotta be done like any other job around here. That's fine by me. And besides, that pelt'll look good over the mantel."

The rancher nodded in reply. Still, it was pretty clear that something was on his son's mind. If not the hunt, what was it? He turned in his saddle and looked up the trail. They'd need to get moving in few minutes if they wanted to get to their favorite campsite before dark. First, though, he thought he'd take another go at figuring out what was troubling the boy. He unslung his canteen and took a long drink, then handed it over to his son. The boy drank deeply, wiped his mouth on his sleeve, and returned the canteen.

The rancher was not much of a conversationalist. In fact, his wife would say that he had a parsimonious relationship with words; he spent as few of them as a man could while still managing to communicate his meaning. He didn't exactly resort to short grunts to get his points across, but, if a glance or shrug could get the message across, well, so much the better. Right now though, sitting on a horse on the side of a mountain as the sun slipped behind the granite peak, plain old-fashioned, out-of-the-dictionary words were called for. He rested his hands on the pommel of his saddle.

"You're troubled, boy," he said. It wasn't a question.

"Yes, I guess you could say I am, but it ain't about the cat. Nothing like that at all."

"Lay it out for me, son," said the rancher. "It's just us up here."

The boy looked high into the sky, then at the rocky ground around his horse's hooves before he spoke.

"It ain't fair. That's what's got me bothered. It ain't fair and it won't ever be fair and I am danged if I know why you are doing what you are doing."

Now the rancher tipped his own hat back. He started to reach for his fixin's only to realize he'd left his tobacco on a fence post down at the remuda. He sighed.

"Well now, son, I'm guessing I could give you a mighty long list of things in this world that don't come within rifle shot distance of being fair, startin' with the ache I got in my shoulder from that musket ball at Chancellorsville and ending with the fact that I have to listen to Mrs. Cady wheeze and whine like a broken furnace bellows through the hymns in front of your mom and me at church. Every Sunday. Five years running. That, son, is what 'not fair' means to me."

The rancher got the grin he hoped for. But only a small one.

"How 'bout you just up and tell me what's got your dander up, son."

The boy glanced up and the rancher saw tears welling in his eyes. He struggled to hold them back. Then, the words burst from his mouth and hit his father with the force of a rattlesnake strike.

"You're going to let the bank take our ranch," he said. "You're gonna let them take it, and you ain't gonna fight, and that's wrong, and you know it's wrong."

The boy had never in his life back-talked his father. He had never disputed any decision the rancher made or second-guessed how his father ran the spread. He respected his father with all his heart. But this, this was a stand he had to take, no matter the consequence.

The rancher's eyes narrowed. He looked closely at his son in the fading light and saw him as he had never seen him before. There had been a similar moment a few years go with the boy's older brother, a single slice of conversation, just a few words really, spoken by the older brother with the same kind of sincerity and conviction as the rancher was hearing now from his youngest boy.

His boy. No, the rancher thought, that wasn't quite right. Not any more. His boy had just stepped across the line from childhood to being a man. It was time to respond in kind.

The rancher wheeled his horse around and edged closer to his son. They were now only about a foot apart. The young man's jaw was clenched, his hands gripped the reins tightly. He wouldn't be backing down from what he had just said, the rancher was sure of that. The rancher couldn't help himself. He shook his head, and then he smiled at his son.

The boy looked at him as if he were crazy.

"Pa, did you hear what I said?"

His father laid his hand on his son's shoulder and spoke with surprising softness. "I heard you. You think I'm doing the wrong thing for honoring my deal with the bank. You think that if I can't sell all of them cows at a decent price, sell them now to pay the note, that if I don't have the payment as I agreed that it's all right for me to just spit in the banker's eye and tell him my word was no good. That about the way you see things?"

His son pulled off his hat and slapped some of the dust from it before answering.

"No, I'm not talking about your word. I'm talking about our home. The place we have all worked our tails off for years to build. Remember the flash flood? The fire that took the barn and the brood mare when she was the only cash resource we had? Them White Mountain Apaches that was tearing things up when we first got here? The bank didn't fight them off. The bank didn't put out that fire or fix things after the flood. We did, with the sweat of our brows and the muscles in our backs, as Ma always says."

The young man sat ramrod straight in his saddle as he talked. The rancher knew that was a sign of respect and another indicator that his son was going to make a fine man.

He replied in slow, measured tones. "Wish I had my fixin's son, I really do. A man naturally talks better when his hands are occupied with the tobacco. Least-wise that's true for me."

A red-tailed hawk swooped low across the face of the mountain right in front of them, riding lazily on the late afternoon air currents. The rancher scratched his horse's jaw. The animal loved that.

"You said something mighty big, and mighty important a minute ago son," the rancher began. "How'd you put it... 'it ain't about your word, Pa, it's about our home.' That pretty much the way you meant for it to come out?"

His son nodded. That's exactly what he meant to say.

"And by that I expect you mean that us keeping the ranch is more important than me keeping my word? That about right, too?"

"It's our HOME, Pa," his son said. "What's more important than our home? You just shook hands with that banker, that ain't no big deal. Pay him later when we are on our feet. He's the richest man in town—a little waitin' won't do him any harm."

The rancher lowered his head in silent thought. Then he turned his horse around and walked back to the edge of the slope. His son followed.

"All of that down there," said the rancher as he swept his arm in a long arc across the sky, "every bit of it, is just things. Stuff. God made the land, we just took a little lumber and put up some buildings and gathered some cattle and some horses and made ourselves a temporary place. I say temporary because nothing made by a man will last forever. That make sense?"

His son acknowledged the point with a shrug of his shoulders.

"Now, I ain't a preacher, and this sure ain't no sermon," the rancher continued, "but there is something each of us carries inside us that ain't temporary like those buildings down below. It's eternal. It's our soul, but it's more than that, too. See son, I care about that ranch every bit as much as you do. So does your Ma and your brother. It's a fine thing we have built, and it's a fine place for me to rest my tired bones every night; but, son, our real home is inside here."

The rancher put his hand over his heart. His son shook his head. He didn't understand.

"Son, your real home isn't built with lumber and stone. It's built with honesty, and character. It's made from integrity and honor. And all of those high and mighty sounding things are protected under the best roof and grounded on the strongest foundation of all. Together they are infinitely stronger and more lasting than them adobe clay shingles on our little house down there. Your word is the foundation, son. And the roof, too. Your word holds it all together come hell or high water. It can't be stolen or repossessed. Nobody can make you give it up, and no amount of money in the world can buy it."

A purplish glow was beginning to spread across the valley below them. It was getting cold, and the horses were starting to paw a little at the ground. They were ready to be unsaddled and staked out in the tall grass to feed.

The young man had never heard his father string so many words together in one conversation in his entire life. Just as his father had looked at him with a new regard a few minutes ago, so, too, did he see his father in a new light.

"Just one last thing, son," said the rancher as he straightened his saddle bag. "You said that the banker was the richest man in town. It's true that he has the most money. But he ain't the richest. All the contracts and mortgages in the world can't make a man truly rich. To be truly rich don't take a single copper penny. All it takes is that each time you shake a man's hand on a deal, or make a promise to your child or stand up for your wife the way you said you would. When you do those things, remember: Your word is your bond. It is the source of your true riches. It is everything you have right now, and it is everything you will ever have."

With that the rancher started his horse back to the trail. His son followed, deep in thought about the conversation they had just finished.

As they started around the next switchback leading up to the campsite, the rancher turned in his saddle.

"And son, just for the record, I've got no intention of letting us lose the ranch. We'll do what we have always done and figure out a way to make the payment on time and with our heads held high. Part of that means you and me had better find that mountain lion pronto and get his hide away from the cattle and up on the mantel."

"Thanks, Pa," said the young man. "You know you can count on me to do my job."

The rancher tapped his spur against his horse's flank and picked up the pace. They'd have to get the lead out if they wanted to make the campsite before dark.

"Keep your word son," the rancher called back as they rode up the mountain in the gathering twilight. "The rest will fall into place."

Introduction

REX TILLERSON SPENT MANY OF HIS BOYHOOD AFTERNOONS ON HIS BICYCLE, racing around the Oklahoma college town his family called home. He played football and baseball, went to church, and was an active Boy Scout. Rex was in all respects an ordinary boy, one who would go on to run the largest company in the world.

He was named after two of the most famous movie cowboys of all time—Rex Allen and John Wayne. He loved Western movies, and to this day appreciates the clear and unambiguous values their heroes stood for. One of those values is that your word is your bond. That principle played a major role in Rex Tillerson's development as a person and as a leader.

As a young boy, he met Rex Allen (who was also famous as the narrator of many Disney films) when his father took him to the Santa Rosa Roundup rodeo in Vernon, Texas, where Allen put on a roping and riding show. When Allen rode around the arena at the end of the show to greet his fans, Rex's dad told the cowboy that his 6-year-old son was named for the Western hero. Allen autographed a scrap of paper for young Rex. Today, Rex Wayne Tillerson has a photograph of Rex Allen on his dresser.

His family moved several times around Texas and Oklahoma during his youth. They were financially comfortable, but by no means were they affluent. The reality of their modest circumstances was not lost on young Rex, and from an early age he was determined to earn his own spending money. He mowed lawns, bused restaurant tables, washed dishes, and worked as a janitor. He discovered early on that he liked work. It provided him a sense of accomplishment and personal satisfaction. Work provided him the opportunity to experience and be tested on the values he learned from his parents and other important people in his life.

He cherishes memories of the summers that he spent working as a counselor at a Boy Scout camp in the country, far from the noise and congestion of the city. In fact, he worked as the director of aquatics at the summer camp until the beginning of his junior year in college. Today, "my Boy Scout values are what I stand on everywhere I go," he says. "As long as I don't lose sight of those, I don't have any problems."[1]

Everything about the Scouting experience made an indelible impression on Rex: the leaders, the friends he made, the campouts and the outdoor adventures that every new summer promised, each in its own way helped to shape the man he would become. The fact that Scouting provided him the opportunity to do things his family could not have afforded on their own is something that has inspired him to support Scouting throughout the years. He wants other boys to have the life-changing kinds of experiences that Scouting provided him.

For Rex, hiking, camping, swimming, working on merit badges, and sharing campfire camaraderie with his fellow Scouts was the beginning of a lifelong appreciation for the natural world. To this day, he says, there is nothing he enjoys more than sitting in a bow blind in a tree in the pre-dawn of a crisp fall morning, watching and listening as the sun comes up and the world comes alive. These were magical experiences for him when he was a young boy, and they are just as powerful for him today whether is he walking alone along a leafy path at his ranch or joining with good friends and their trusted retrievers for a morning of wing shooting.

In high school he was a percussionist in the marching band. In its own way this was a leadership role: the entire band had to march to the beat of his drum. The time he spent honing his marching band skills paid off in more ways than one; when he was accepted as a freshman at University of Texas, Austin, to study civil engineering, a scholarship helped pave the way, and he became a member of the famous UT Longhorn Band.

Rex distinguished himself in his leadership role with the marching band's 320 members, but he acknowledges that he was not an outstanding scholar. His grades were solid, though, and as he neared completion of his civil engineering degree during his final year at UT, he was recruited by firms from several different industries. The job offers were attractive, and he labored over the choice of which company to choose. He told the recruiters from Exxon—the company that was pursuing him the hardest—that he didn't know anything about the oil business. It seems the recruiters saw enough promise in Rex that his lack of familiarity with their business wasn't an issue. Join us, they said, and you can learn on the job. In the end, he chose Exxon, and joined them as a production engineer in 1975.

He rapidly ascended the ranks within Exxon. By 1989 he was the general manager of the Exxon USA central production division. In this role he was responsible for oil and gas operations across much of Oklahoma, Texas, Kansas, and Arkansas. His roles and responsibilities in the company expanded rapidly; in 1992 he became the Exxon Corporation's production advisor, and in 1995 he was named president of Exxon Yemen, Esso Exploration, and Production Khorat. His experience was broadened with responsibilities in Russia and the Caspian Sea (including offshore operations at Sakhalin Island, Russia) when he became vice president of Exxon Ventures (CIS), and president of Exxon Neftegas Limited. His leadership roles increased when he became executive vice president of ExxonMobil Development Corporation in 2000, and senior vice president of ExxonMobil Corporation in 2001. In 2004 Rex Tillerson was elected president of the corporation and a member of the board of directors. Finally, he became chairman and chief executive officer on January 1, 2006.

His tenure at the head of the world's largest company has been marked by extraordinary successes and a noticeable change in style and tone, in particular in regard to how Rex has worked to build better relationships with stakeholders, partners, customers, the media, and the public at large. He is acutely aware of the array of critics and naysayers who fervently oppose almost any initiative his company—or almost any energy company for that matter—undertakes. Tillerson's response to those voices has been to reinforce and strengthen ExxonMobil's focus on ethical corporate behavior and to forge global, regional, and local partnerships with companies that do the same. He has been a highly visible and communicative CEO who understands that public opinion is best shaped in an atmosphere of transparency.

An example of his leadership style took place early in his tenure when Rex sat down for an unprecedented interview with *The New York Times* in which he stated that his company knew that climate was changing, the average temperature of the Earth was rising, and greenhouse gas emissions were increasing. His statement was really nothing new: in fact, his company had been talking about it for some time. Even so, the article that appeared in the *Times* after the interview suggested that Tillerson's statement was a major shift in his company's attitude about climate change. "If Rex W. Tillerson has his way," the *Times* article began, "ExxonMobil will no longer be the oil company that environmentalists love to hate."[2]

He has made the argument to both the Bush and the Obama administrations that achieving energy security is far more important than the goal of achieving energy independence. It is the global marketplace, he argues, that actually promises the most effective means of achieving U.S. energy security—the nationality of the resources are of little relevance.

Under Tillerson's leadership, ExxonMobil gained access to more oil fields from the United Arab Emirates to Guyana. Even as the company continued to pursue the growth and development of traditional fossil fuel resources around the globe, Rex also made research into alternative and cleaner energy sources a priority. In 2009, for example, ExxonMobil announced its intention to invest $600 million to produce liquid transportation fuels from algae—organisms in water ranging from pond scum to seaweed. Two years later, Tillerson oversaw the multibillion-dollar purchase of XTO Energy, a major producer of natural gas.

Natural gas is an abundant, cleaner energy source that is an extraordinarily important component of the world's available energy mix. Early in his career, Tillerson played a hands-on role in helping to develop the hydraulic fracturing techniques that make accessing and using that natural gas possible. The process is currently used in most of the natural gas wells in the United States. Hydraulic fracturing pumps treated water and sand underground, which breaks apart the rock and releases the gas. It is a very successful production technique, but one that has been the subject of continuing controversy. Tillerson recognizes the challenge of educating and informing the public about this process. Once people have accurate information based on independent scientific research about hydraulic fracturing, he is confident that most people will accept the process as a safe and reliable means for delivering more energy to millions of people.

The fact of the matter is, Tillerson says, humanity is going to continue to depend on hydrocarbons as a primary energy source for the forseeable future. Those fuels not only underpin the world's manufacturing, transportation, farming, distribution, housing, and health sectors, but they are also the only pathway to a better life for the hundreds of millions of people around the world who live in abject poverty. He argues that the first response to the recognition that fossil fuels have an impact on the environment, *and* that these fuels will eventually be exhausted, should be to dramatically improve our energy *efficiency*. Other solutions and new technologies are being developed today, and more and more will become reliable, efficient, and affordable over time. Right now, he says, we need to work with what we have even as we research new solutions.

Being the head of the largest company in the world has kept Rex Tillerson in the public spotlight for many years. *Forbes Magazine* has named him one of the most powerful people in the world every year since he took the helm at ExxonMobil.[3] That recognition doesn't mean a lot to Rex. He likes to point out—usually with a chuckle—that people think he is smarter than he really is. In fact, he says, he is just a regular guy. He says that when his minister asks how he deals with the avalanche of worldwide attention that comes his way—both the positive and the negative—his answer is to point out how important it is to never lose sight of who you are, what you believe in, and what you hold to be true. For Rex, that includes his belief that the Lord put him where he is for a reason, as we are all where we are for a reason—even if we are sometimes not so sure ourselves.

"Just don't ever think it's all about you," he says. "Don't think that you're bigger than anything around you, because you're not, and it'll all play out if you just do the right things."[4]

In the pages that follow, Rex W. Tillerson shares the account of his development as a leader, including many of the major decisions he has made as chairman and CEO of the largest and most successful company in the world.

---

[1] Personal interviews with Rex Tillerson, 13 July, 2012 and 30 July, 2012.

[2] Mouawad, Jad. "The New Face of an Oil Giant." *The New York Times.* 30 March, 2006.

[3] Forbes' Powerful People List. www.forbes.com/profile/rex-tillerson

[4] Personal interviews with Rex Tillerson, 13 July, 2012 and 30 July, 2012

I

I WAS BORN IN A TWO-BEDROOM FRAME HOUSE in a community called Faith Village in Wichita Falls, Texas. My family didn't have a lot, but that didn't really matter—it was a very happy home to grow up in. I had two sisters, one older and one younger. I was in the middle, the proverbial ham in the sandwich.

My mom and dad married after he came home from his Navy service during World War II. His first job after the war was driving a bread truck and making sales to grocery stores.

Other than my family and church, the biggest influence in my early life was the Boy Scouts of America. The BSA was a huge part of my upbringing because Scouting meant so much to my father. When he went off to the war he was 17, and he had not completed his Eagle Scout requirements. By the time he got back, he was over 18; under ordinary circumstances that would have meant that he had missed the cut off and he wouldn't have been able to finish. But the BSA had a program after World War II that granted an extension to men who had gone to the war before their 18th birthday. If they wanted to complete their Eagle Scout requirements, the exemption made it possible. After the war he took up again with his troop as an assistant Scoutmaster and went on to finish the requirements for earning the rank of Eagle Scout. At his court of honor, he received the badge alongside two younger boys from his troop. He was a Vigil Honor member of the Order of the Arrow, and he was a head of the dance team. My father was all about Scouting for his entire life.

My earliest memories of Scouting are trips to Camp Perkins outside of Wichita Falls for the Friday evening campfires when I was a toddler. We used to watch the dance team perform traditional American Indian dances. That just captivated me. When I was about 6, a professional Scouter from that council approached my dad and said, "You seem to really have a passion for Scouting. Have you ever thought about doing it for a profession?" My dad took him up on the offer. He went to work for the Boy Scouts, even though it meant taking a pay cut from his bread sales job. His first assignment as a district executive was in Vernon, Texas, about an hour's drive up along the Red River from Wichita Falls. That's where I started elementary school, and where I joined the Cub Scouts when I turned 8.

We moved again just a year later when my dad took another district executive assignment, this time in Stillwater, Oklahoma, with the Will Rogers Council. We lived there for about eight years, which was the longest period of time I ever lived anywhere while I was growing up. The heart of my Scouting experience was in Stillwater; I finished my Cub Scouting, joined a Boy Scout troop, became an Explorer, and worked on the camp staff. Those were phenomenal experiences for me in my formative years.

With the nature of the profession being what it is, my dad was gone most nights training volunteers, organizing units, meeting with chartered organizations, and so on. He wasn't around a lot when I was growing up. In all the years I played baseball he might have made it to two or three of my Little League games. I don't recall if he ever came to any of my football games, maybe one or two of them. He was gone all the time. That was the job.

My mom was central to my growing up because she did pretty much everything. Many of the personal characteristics and attributes that have helped me the most throughout my life came to me from her. She was always confident in us, and she was an example of what it meant to be self-confident. She valued family so much, and she lived by a strong set of values.

She had to deal with many difficulties when I was young. While still a young mother with three children to take care of, for example, her own mother became ill. And only a couple of years after grandmother passed, my mother's father died. They had both been in their early 50s. When grandfather died, my aunt, my mother's youngest sister, who was still in high school, moved in with us.

That meant my mom was trying to raise a family with three young kids on a pretty meager income. She lost both of her parents in a short time period, and then she took in her younger sister. It was a lot to deal with, and she did it without much help. Even so, during those formative years, and right to this day, she was a model of emotional strength, and a huge influence on the development of my attitude toward hard work and the importance of a positive outlook. "Never give up." "Don't ever let anybody get you down." "Just work through it, and as long as you're working on the right things, everything will turn out just fine." Those are the sorts of things that defined her then just as they do now. Her positive attitude had a lasting impact on me. I don't ever let things get me down.

My minister once said, "Rex, I don't understand how you do what you do." That's a fair statement given the kinds of people I sometimes have to deal with, and the pressure of those situations, plus the fact that I have multiple difficult and complex situations that I am responsible for overseeing every day. In my job, I don't necessarily have the luxury of finishing off one situation and closing the book on it knowing that it will go away never to bother me again. When we're operating in 60 or 70 countries around the world as we do at ExxonMobil, a lot of situations come up. In fact, in some of those places, the word "country" isn't an accurate description, because some of the states are brand new with equally new governments in place.

That can make for quite a bit of uncertainty, and in my job you have to deal with all of it. In some situations you may even have your people at risk, and you certainly have your company's assets on the line. How do I deal with that kind of pressure?

Believe it or not, I don't lose sleep over it. In my experience I have found that if you possess a strong set of values to guide what you do every day, and if you don't ever vary from those values, and if you focus on doing the best job you can, things will turn out. Don't worry about the things that are outside of your control. Work on the things you *can* control.

Of course, even when you stick to your principles and do your best to do the right things for the people you are both responsible for and accountable to, that doesn't guarantee success in a given endeavor. You are not always going to be successful. Every one of your projects is not going to be a complete winner; but, as my mom used to point out, if you're not experiencing some failures you're probably not trying hard enough. That was an important lesson for me when I was growing up. She encouraged me to do anything I ever wanted to do, even if I wasn't any good at it. I don't remember her ever saying "no" to me on anything that I wanted to do, or that I thought I might pursue. She always did her best to support my efforts when I wanted to try something new, even if there wasn't one chance in 1,000 that I was going to be successful at it. Her belief was that it was important to go out and experience new things, and if they didn't turn out the way you expected or wanted, well then, you got an opportunity to learn to deal with failure and disappointment, and that experience is critical for success in all aspects of life, business and personal. Failure isn't the end of the world, and so you shouldn't let it get you down. Pick yourself up and move on to the next thing.

When we moved to Stillwater, my mother went to work, which was pretty unusual for a married mother of three in those days. My parents hadn't been able to make financial ends meet raising three kids while living in a college town where the cost of living was higher. So mom went to work, and my sisters and I became latchkey kids. It was fortunate that the house we lived in was directly across the street from the elementary school. My little sister and I would just walk across the street and walk back home, and then wait for Mom to get home from work.

I had a bicycle, and in those days, it was safe to take off. I rode all over Stillwater. I'd ride miles across town to where I went to junior high school. I had a friend whom I would meet on the corner and away we'd go. There was a great sense of freedom in that. The experience of my mom going to work, flying everywhere on my bike, and waiting for Mom to come home all had a significant impact on me.

Church was another major influence in my early years. My parents were very active in our church, and I participated in all the youth organizations. The first thing I did when I became a Boy Scout was earn my God and Country Award. That took about 18 months. The pastor didn't just hand those awards out. He really made you earn it. I was there nearly every Sunday afternoon to meet with him at 3:00, and then youth fellowship would start at 5:00. I'd spend almost the entire day in church each Sunday because I sang in the youth choir. I'd be there for the 8:00 a.m. church service with the youth choir, then I'd go to Sunday School, and then I was an usher at the 11:00 liturgy to fulfill the service requirement of my God and Country Award. That meant going to church twice, then to lunch before jumping on my bike and pedaling back to church for my 3:00 session with my minister for the award. When we finished up around 4:00 or 4:30 I'd hang around the church until youth fellowship started at 5:00. That was over at 6:30, when I was finally able to go home. I pretty much spent all day each Sunday at church.

From my vantage point today, I realize we had very little in the way of money or possessions when I was young. At the time I never even thought about it. It registered more with my older sister as she was dealing with that reality during her high school years. It was tough on her. My little sister and I were blissfully unaware of the fact that we didn't have a lot. We grew up having a great time in a warm, close-knit family.

2

I HAVE ALWAYS BEEN A GREAT FAN OF OUR WESTERN HERITAGE. I love old western movies, and I grew up watching "The Lone Ranger" and "The Cisco Kid" on TV. I grew up in an era where it was easy to tell the good guys from the bad guys. Right and wrong were pretty clearly defined black-and-white notions, and there weren't too many gray areas. The two cowboy stars I was named for, Rex Allen and John Wayne, both played those kinds of roles throughout their careers. Maybe life was a little simpler back in that post-World War II era. Maybe it wasn't. Either way, the truth is that it was clear who the good guy was and who the bad guy was. Right was right and wrong was wrong, and there were no ifs, ands, or buts about it.

I still look at right and wrong in a straightforward, uncomplicated way. The cowboy values that I saw depicted in the shows I loved watching as a boy had something to do with my outlook, and so did my parents, school, church, and Scouting, which was a constant in my formative years. In Scouting I learned so much about life, about pushing myself to do my best, and about leadership, perseverance, teamwork, and the difference between right and wrong.

I was 8 years old when I joined Cub Scouts. I had the opportunity to learn a lesson about right and wrong at one of my first pack meetings. An older boy started picking on me when we were outside the church.

Then he started shoving me. I didn't know what to do. I had never had anybody shove me around before. I didn't know whether I should try to fight him or run away. Right about that moment, my mom walked up. She saw me getting shoved around, and she put a stop to it. I was really embarrassed. In fact, I cried because it embarrassed me so much, but my mother took me aside and did something remarkable. She brought up the Cub Scout Promise and the Law of the Pack, and talked about what's right, what's wrong, and how sometimes you have to fight; but sometimes the right thing to do is to just walk away. It was the other boy who had lost, she pointed out; he damaged his own reputation because now everybody knew he was a bully.

That was quite a teachable moment for an 8-year-old. There would be more to come—too many to count—in the years that followed, of course. Life is filled with such moments. Scouting presented me with so many opportunities for growth, as an individual, and as a member of a group. I do think that too much is made about the importance of teaching leadership, however. To be sure, the leadership training that is provided in Scouting helps young men to build the self-esteem and self-confidence they need to deal with the world they're going to have to live in as adults. That's why the leadership experiences are so important. As I look back on my Scouting experience, though, even accounting for the fact that I have ended up in some pretty important leadership positions in my life, I realize that the thing I learned most in Scouting was good *followership*, and how important it was to be a good patrol member. In particular I learned how important it was to support the people who were trying to lead you. If you did that— and the other members of your team did, too—things just went well.

It was critical for my own development that I learned as much or more about followership as I did about leadership. They're inextricably linked. Great leaders understand what it takes to get people to follow them.

That's what the term "leader" means—when you turn around you want to see everybody following you. Leadership is getting others behind you and keeping them there. In my experience, the key to leadership is truly and deeply understanding what good followership is. "How did I feel when I was being a good follower? What made me want to be a good follower? What made me want to follow that person?" That's what I needed to understand as a leader.

In Scouting I got to experience being a part of a genuine team effort, where no one person could make the whole thing work on his own. It had to happen through the collective efforts of everybody, even the weakest member. When everyone worked together, truly extraordinary things were possible, even in the face of extreme mental and physical challenges— successes that no individual could achieve on his own. The high adventure experiences I had as a boy at Charles L. Sommers Canoe Base and Philmont cemented that understanding in my mind.

At those demanding moments when you look around at your crew you have to take stock and ask yourself, where is everybody? Where's my weak link? What do I want to do about the weak link? Do I beat him like a horse and berate him and goad him into pulling his weight? Or do I want to support him and push him from behind without him even knowing I'm pushing him?

When I went to Sommers Canoe Base, I was the weak link in my crew. At least I felt like I was. I was barely 14 years old, which meant I was just at the eligibility line for attending. I probably weighed 85 or 90 pounds soaking wet. We were trekking with those old waxed-canvas Duluth packs, and 19-foot aluminum Grumman canoes.

The canoes weighed 90 pounds, about what I did. They had a wooden yoke in the middle with two foam pads, and before we set out from base camp we were trained in loading the canoe onto our shoulders. That was a precarious business. You waded into the water, rolled it up on your waist, and then used leverage to get it up on your shoulders. Imagine this giant 19-foot canoe rocking up and down on your shoulders like a teeter-totter while you tried to get it balanced just right so that you could lug the thing a quarter-mile through mud that came halfway up your ankles.

Three of us were assigned to each canoe. At every portage, one person carried the canoe, one person carried the food pack, and one person carried the gear pack. Then we would rotate tasks at the next portage.

I had gotten pretty good at hoisting the canoe up onto my shoulders during training. So, when we got to the first portage where I was to carry the canoe, I was proud of myself because I got it raised up and balanced on my own. I came out of the water with it, and we took off down a trail. I don't remember how long the portage actually was, and I don't know how far into it we were—probably only 100 yards—but I was dying. I couldn't see where I was going. I was afraid I was going to trip and fall. With each step it became clearer that I couldn't do it. I was overwhelmed physically, and I thought I was about to have an emotional breakdown.

"I can't do this," I said. "I can't do this."

The group came to a halt. My crew chief and the ranger approached me. I was standing there, shaking, trying my best not to drop the canoe. They popped their heads underneath the canoe so they could make eye contact with me.

"You can do this," they said. "Just keep walking."

I tried. I took five or six more steps, but that's all I had in me. I was sure I was about to have a mental breakdown right on the spot.

They lifted the canoe off of my shoulders, and took a break so I could regroup. The others tried their best to motivate me. Then my two canoe partners said they would help me. "We'll all get under it and carry it together."

That's when the crew chief looked at me and said, "Is that really what you want to do?"

I wasn't sure how to answer him. I took a sip of water and tried to gather myself together. My partners offered again to help carry the canoe, while my crew chief kept looking at me with an expression that said, "Well, do what you want to do."

"No," I finally said, "No. I'll do it." They helped me to get the canoe back up, and away we went. I made it all the way. I thought I was going to die before dinnertime that day, but the others didn't hear a peep out of me after that. I put one foot in front of the other, kept focused, and didn't have another problem.

I was the weak link that day, but I had been able to rally and push through. That was huge for me in terms of my self-confidence. I didn't give up that day, and I didn't allow myself to get overwhelmed. Even though I was small, I realized I could do it. And I did. From then on, I knew I could do anything.

When I was 16, I went to Philmont on a backpacking trek with my Explorer post. The hike over Baldy is one of the most difficult at Philmont, and the heat made it worse. Switchback after switchback we were steadily hiking toward the summit, and now we were running behind schedule. Because you're exposed to the elements when you're summiting and starting your descent down the opposite side, it's important that you get up there and then get clear before it's too late in the day, when lightning strikes are common.

We weren't keeping the pace that we needed that day because we had our own weak link, an exhausted, overwhelmed 14-year-old Scout. At every switchback, he'd sit down. I looked at my watch and saw that we were getting farther and farther behind. Then I thought back on what happened to me two years earlier during the canoe portage. I told everybody to take a water break and walked over to the Scout who was holding things up.

He was a mirror image of what I had been on the canoe trip, including being on the verge of having an emotional breakdown. I gave him some time. Some of the guys were grumbling and getting ready to start calling him names. I told them to cool it.

I went back to the Scout and offered him a way out: "If you want, we can see if we can get some of the other guys to carry some of your stuff. We can take some of the weight out of your pack and redistribute it."

On cue, a couple of the older guys stepped forward and said, "I'll take some."

He looked up and said, "Yeah, maybe that's what I should do."

"Why don't you think about that a little," I said before walking away to give him a minute. When I went back to him a second time I said, "You know, we still have three or four more days to go before we get in. This will be the hardest day. This is as hard as it gets. What do you think?"

He took a deep breath, and started putting his pack back on. "Let's go," he said, "Let's just go." He never sat down again.

I don't know exactly what was going through his mind at that point. Maybe he needed time to regroup. Maybe he was inspired by the fact that he had a couple of buddies that were ready to help him and would have. Maybe it was just the knowledge, the reassurance that said, "Okay, I'm not in this alone, I'm not going to die. We're all going to make it together." More than likely it was a combination of all of those things. That's how it had worked for me a couple years earlier. And now, it worked for him.

Those were great lessons for me about being part of a team. They were great lessons about leadership, too, but also great lessons about the importance of knowing when and how to follow. There was something universal in those life lessons, something was genuinely applicable to the issues I faced in my day-to-day life. That sense of self-confidence combined with the ability to know how to work well with others really came in handy when my family had to deal with relocating again. Over Thanksgiving holiday in 1968 my family moved to Huntsville, Texas, when my father was transferred. We had felt settled in Stillwater, but it wasn't to be. It was a disruptive move for me because I was in the middle of my junior year. Suddenly I was plunked down in a new environment surrounded by unfamiliar people.

Even in the chaos of moving and starting over with a school and new friends, there was still an important system of continuity, something familiar I could plug myself into no matter where I went: Scouting. It helped me make the transition. The Boy Scout troop I belonged to in Stillwater had been just phenomenal. If you were to write the textbook on the perfect Scout troop, it could have served as the model. It was distinguished by excellent leadership, strong spirit, and efficient organization from the Scoutmaster on down. It was a privilege to be a part of that troop. I knew that there was no way my new troop in Huntsville could be my old troop's equal.

Even so, what my new troop was not able to provide on its own, Scouting as a broader movement provided to me in spades. In the summer of 1969, between my junior and senior year of high school, I was a part of a contingent that went to the national jamboree in Idaho. I was 17, and it was the first time I'd ever been on an airplane. We flew out of Houston up to Farragut State Park, Idaho, where the jamboree was held. Coming home we took a bus tour that stopped at Yellowstone National Park before winding down through the middle of the country back to Houston. The whole thing was quite an adventure.

The jamboree experience was particularly memorable for another reason: the Apollo 11 crew reached the moon while the jamboree was going on. We were able to watch that momentous broadcast live and to see Neil Armstrong and Buzz Aldrin become the first human beings to walk on the surface of the moon. Neil Armstrong was an Eagle Scout, which made the event even more powerful and personal to each of us there. In fact, at one point Armstrong broadcast a special message from space to those of us at the jamboree. It was an enthralling moment. We were camped at Farragut State Park in Idaho at the same time that two American astronauts were on the moon. More incredibly, one of those astronauts—himself an Eagle Scout—was speaking to us Scouts directly. It was almost surreal, a bit hard to process. It was very special and very inspiring.

Science had always been interesting to me, but now, like countless other young people who witnessed the exploits of those astronauts, I felt inspired to pursue the sciences at a higher level. The moon landing was one of the major inspirations in my becoming an engineer.

Neil Armstrong himself was a compelling figure and an exemplary man. Interestingly enough, after the seemingly personal experience of receiving a special greeting from Armstrong from outer space—one that I shared with about 35,000 other jamboree attendees—he was the commencement speaker at my college graduation six years later.

A few years ago, not long before he died, I was privileged to meet Neil Armstrong in person. We had a little time to talk. I shared my story of being in Farragut State Park as a Scout at the jamboree. I told him that it meant so much to me as a young man to receive that special greeting from him in outer space, that it felt like a personal message, that it inspired me and told me that almost anything was possible.

Armstrong smiled. "You can't believe the thousands of men I've run into," he said, "that told me they were there, too."

He was a modest man, and wonderful example to all young people. He could have capitalized on his fame and cashed in, but such action would have violated his personal value system. Other astronauts didn't hesitate to seek the adulation and material wealth that was offered to them because they had served their country and the cause of science by going to space, but Armstrong—a man who could have taken advantage of that like few other figures of the 20th century—chose not to. I've always wondered if his Scouting experience had something to do with that. One of the things Scouting teaches is that achieving the goal is never up to one person. Instead, mileposts are reached and the race is won through the collective efforts of a unified group of people working together toward one goal.

Yes, you may be responsible for and enjoy some success as an individual, but broadly speaking you should not make that story all about you. You did not get there all by yourself. If you do try to make it about you, you diminish the important role that many other people played in the story. I want people to be proud that I achieved what I did, knowing that they played some part in the story, too. It's never about one person. Success is a product of many, even when the light shines on just one.

3

TEAMWORK MATTERS everywhere. In addition to Scouting I participated in sports, and there, too, it was all about being an individual part of a larger whole. I was an average athlete. I did my time in games, but I was never a star. I chalk that up partly to ability and partly to desire. I didn't dedicate myself to sports the way some of the other guys did. Still, there wasn't a question of whether or not to participate; all of my peers played, so I did as well.

I've always found the whole idea of the "superstar" athlete to be interesting. It often seems as if our whole sports culture, from coaches to commentators to the fans and the players themselves, revolves around and emphasizes the unique importance of the star. That's generally where the recognition and the attention goes, no matter the sport. In that sense, sports serves as a kind of microcosm for life.

Fans want to see their team win, but, almost even more than that, they want to see the star. That's why they come. In football, most people can't name the individual players on the offensive line, but they can almost always name the running back and the quarterback, and probably the wide receiver. Most people can't name very many of the defensive players either, but the plain truth is that the team won't win unless all of those roles are performed well and in unison. The superstars themselves aren't enough to get the job done.

Scouting provides a different model. The concept of rotating leadership means that everybody takes a turn at being the star, to the extent that you could refer to anyone in a troop as a "star." The patrol leader, the senior patrol leader, the OA lodge chief—no boy that rises to one of these positions holds it in perpetuity. They rotate and then they go back into the ranks. One day you're the senior patrol leader, the boy responsible for directing the entire troop, and the very next day next you're back in the ranks.

That's a far cry from the attitude that dominates athletics. The objective there is simple: to win the game. When you win a game, you put a big "W" in the win column and then you get ready to go out to the next game and do it again. That's why in sports you are only as good as your last game. In Scouting, on the other hand, every game stays with you. Nothing gets thrown away. Everything you do has a purpose and a meaning that is greater than the accomplishment on any single day.

Scouting operates like a continuum. Every rank advancement, and every group activity or outing, is tied together. There is a string that connects them all. Maybe you don't recognize it at the time. At some point in your life, though, you become aware of the rock-solid foundation that underpins everything you do. You realize that you truly are prepared for anything the world might throw at you.

Whether you go on to be a leader of a big organization, or a carpenter, or an astronaut, or a roughneck, or a schoolteacher, or an accountant, Scouting is going to make you a better citizen. The Scouting experience attunes you to the perspectives and needs of the people around you.

Nothing ever gets thrown away.

In my formative years the things I excelled at were Scouts and music. I enjoyed the time I spent playing sports, but I was a lot more excited about going to the Boy Scout meeting on Monday night and going camping that month. I couldn't wait to get back to my job on the summer camp staff each year. I excelled at music, both chorally and as a percussionist. In school, I wasn't going to be the valedictorian or salutatorian, but I was a pretty good A-B student. I studied hard and performed near the top of my class in high school.

When it was time to figure out where I would go to college I had already decided that I wanted to go into engineering. The roots of that decision went back to childhood work experiences I had in Stillwater.

My first job was mowing lawns around the neighborhood. I started doing that when I was about 8. If I did a good job I could earn a couple dollars. It didn't take long for me to figure out that mowing lawns wasn't always going to cut it. With our family situation as it was in those days, there wasn't a lot of allowance money, so I supplemented my Scouting expenses with money I earned.

I knew that Oklahoma State hired high school students for various jobs on campus, so I went to the student union and applied to be a busboy. Unfortunately, I was just 13, and you had to be 14 to get hired. A friendly man at the school explained to me that Oklahoma's child labor law didn't allow anyone to work at 13. I'll never forget his name—Mr. Ballou.

"I can't hire you until you turn 14," he said, "and you'll have to get a work permit from the state." He was kind enough to give me the paperwork and to invite me to come back and see him when I turned 14. I couldn't wait.

I returned promptly on my 14th birthday, and sure enough, Mr. Ballou helped me to do the paperwork. My mom had to sign off on it before it was mailed to the Oklahoma Employment Commission. I still have the employment permit the State of Oklahoma sent to me. It's got my teenage signature at the bottom, and today it is framed on the wall of my study.

With permit in hand I started working at Oklahoma State as a busboy. I was paid $0.75 an hour. The number of hours I could work was limited; I worked after school two days a week, from 4:00 until 7:00, and Saturday or Sunday mornings from 11:00 a.m. to 1:00 p.m. busing dishes. If I was really lucky, I got to help load dishes into the big industrial dishwasher. I used to love to load that thing.

I worked as a busboy until I turned 16, which was the age requirement to apply for a job as a janitor. That job paid $1.00 per hour, a huge raise! I was hired, and in short order I was assigned to the electrical engineering building. We worked from 5:00 to 7:00 every evening, and then from 8:00 to 12:00 on Saturdays.

My duties consisted mostly of things like dumping the trash, sweeping the floors, cleaning the bathrooms, and tidying the lecture halls. On the weekends we tackled bigger projects, like buffing the floors, which we couldn't do when there were more people around during the week.

I usually worked on the second floor. One day I got a different assignment: I was going down to the basement where the labs were located. Normally, on my floor, there wouldn't be anybody around while I was cleaning. That day there were several graduate students and other people doing technical work in the lab. I tried my best to sweep around them, to get the trash picked up and in general to stay out of everybody's way. I was pretty curious, and I listened in to some of their conversations as I worked. Whatever they were doing was interesting.

"What are you guys doing?" I finally asked.

They told me that they were engineering students working on an experiment for a class. I was fascinated—and from that day forward, it was engineering for me.

About that time my older sister began dating the young man who would later become my brother-in-law. We had moved down to Huntsville; she was a junior at the University of Texas. I was four years behind her, near the end of high school. She brought her boyfriend home one weekend to meet my parents, and as luck would have it he was a civil engineering major.

He and I sat at the kitchen table one night, and he obliged as I peppered him with questions for two hours. He was in every sense of the word an engineer's engineer. When I was sweeping floors in the engineering lab I was interested; now I was sold completely on the idea of becoming an engineer.

I had my sights set on the University of Texas (UT) by that time. Had we not moved from Oklahoma to Texas, I'm sure I would have gone to Oklahoma State. With our financial situation being what it was, though, I needed to go to an in-state school where tuition was lower than it would be at an out-of-state college. When I applied I also auditioned for the Longhorn Band. Acceptance into the band was a highly competitive process. In fact, they accepted only about half the people who auditioned. I felt honored when I made the cut and was accepted.

I had to take out a student loan so I could afford to go my first year, and I continued to do odd jobs during terms so I had enough money to get by. Later I began to make enough money during summer break that I didn't have to work during the school year. One of the biggest reasons I was able to afford college was the fact that the scholarship I qualified for was only open to band members who happened to be engineering majors. I was both. The Louis T. Wagner Scholarship had been created specifically to help engineers who were in the band because Mr. Wagner worried that engineers had a propensity for sticking to their studies at the expense of their social development. Engineering was a rigorous major and the band was a substantial time commitment—three nights per week, and all weekend long. If you maintained a C average in your classes, and remained in good standing with the band, the scholarship paid a portion of your tuition, fees, and books your first year. Fortunately, the scholarship grew each year. I received the scholarship for four full years, and by the end it paid the complete cost of my tuition, fees, and books.

Being a member of the band was a fantastic experience, and some of the best on-the-job leadership education I have ever received. To this day, I've never had as much fun, even though it was really hard work.

The band director was a remarkable man named Vincent R. DiNino—known to us as Mr. D. When he was hired from Michigan the UT band was just average at best. Mr. D. took on the challenge of turning an average organization into a thriving, nationally recognized spirit organization that came to be known as the Showband of the Southwest.

Mr. D. was a real disciplinarian, and the band practices were as demanding as a perfectionist like him could engineer. He could be brutal. He called me out one night during practice from his perch high in the tower in Memorial Stadium. That night he saw something he didn't like. He bellowed at me through his bullhorn: "Tillerson, get out on the 50-yard line."

He made me stand out in front of everyone while he chewed me out because the tempo wasn't correct, and my responsibility in percussion was to make sure the tempo was exactly right. It had to be perfect for rest of the band to follow. I was the section leader of percussion, and setting the right tempo was my responsibility. I hadn't done my job. Mr D. let me have it in front of 320 of my friends. When he was done, I walked back into line with my tail between my legs.

Despite his reputation for demanding near perfection, Mr. D. loved everybody in the band like they were his family. He would do anything for the members of his band, often without them knowing. Many years after he quietly lent a hand or did a favor for you without you knowing, you would discover what Mr. D did for you. You always wanted to do well for him. You never wanted to let him down.

The UT band was a great support system for me through college. It was the band, especially, that helped me to develop into the leader that I am today. The day I joined I instantly had 320 new friends. There's a lot to be said for that. It was a great experience, and an important part of my university life, along with the Tejas Club, and Alpha Phi Omega (APO), the national coeducational service organization that is founded on the principles of leadership, friendship, and service. My schedule only allowed me to be active in APO for one year, but over the years I have continued to support each of those organizations.

4

I WASN'T A MAGNA CUM LAUDE STUDENT in college. My grades were average, but I worked hard for each one of them. As I approached graduation and began to think about career choices, the fact that my grade-point average didn't place me at the top of my class mattered a heck of a lot less to me than the fact that I had a lot of leadership experience on my résumé.

The year 1975 was a fantastic time to be graduating with an engineering degree. During my final term I received a total of 14 job offers from companies with whom I interviewed. They included chemical companies, engineering firms, construction firms, the government, and a few oil companies. My degree was in civil engineering, and I had completed several hours toward a master's degree. I considered pursuing a graduate degree, but I was facing a number of realities that suggested I had better get a job. First, I was now married; and second, I didn't have any money. In the end the question about graduate school answered itself. In any event, I was ready to get to work. Now I was left with a very difficult decision: Which job offer should I accept?

I had worked the prior summer in Houston on the ship channel for Armco Steel Corporation. They liked me and wanted me to go to work for them. In fact, their offer was the best I received from anybody. They called me regularly, and offered me a high starting salary, a bonus after six months, and a raise. It was an almost irresistible offer. If not for the dogged persuasiveness of the recruiters from a certain oil company, I would have gladly accepted Armco's offer.

However, that oil company—Exxon—just kept after me. They recruited harder than any of the other companies who had offered me a job. In the fall of my senior year I took what they call a plant visit with them, and that's when they offered me the job. As I was trying to sort through all of the job offers I received near the end of the year, I had a hard time figuring out where a guy with a civil engineering degree would fit in an oil company. It was hard for me to see.

When the Exxon recruiters came back over to the campus in February for their spring recruiting, they called me up and said, "We want to take you and your wife out to dinner."

They took us to the fanciest restaurant in Austin. I had never in my life been to any place like that. It scared me; I wasn't sure what silverware to use, or which glass to drink out of. After dinner they drove us back to married student housing where we lived, wished my wife goodnight, and then asked if they could talk with me for a minute.

It was a long minute; they worked me over in that parking lot for an hour and a half. I appreciated their earnestness, but I tried to explain to them that going to work for an oil company just didn't seem like the right fit for me. "I don't understand what I'd be doing," I told them. "I don't know a thing about the oil business. I'm a civil engineer. I know concrete. I know steel, and I know a little about soil mechanics. That's it."

My objections fell on deaf ears: "Don't worry about it," they said, "just come to work. You'll figure it out."

I walked inside that night and told my wife, "You know, these guys *really* want me to work for them." Even though they were offering me a little less money than Armco had, I was finally convinced that taking the job with Exxon was at least worth giving a shot. "I think I'm going to go work for them," I told her. "In one year, we'll take a look back and make an assessment. If it's not going well, I'm pretty sure the guys at Armco will still hire me."

I signed on with Exxon and went right to work. They sent me to the smallest district in Exxon USA—Katy, Texas. Katy was a huge natural gas field west of Houston that also included a small oil field. At that time it was Exxon's second largest natural gas processing plant in the United States and a major hub for natural gas distribution and transmission. Even so, there were only 11 engineers located at Katy. The small size of the engineering staff made it the perfect place for me to get my feet wet—everybody had to do a little bit of everything.

At Katy I learned about natural gas production and drilling. I learned about oil well workovers, oil production, and gas processing. I also learned about plant mechanics. Katy provided me with great grounding in the business—and I received it very quickly.

Even though I was the guy who didn't know much of anything, I was immediately handed responsibilities. Because we were such a small staff, we had weekend duty rotation. Once a month I had to go out and be on duty on Saturday and Sunday. I could go home by noon if nothing was going wrong while remaining on call throughout the weekend if there was a problem. Those weekend rotations gave me the opportunity to travel the area with the wage earners, the process operators and pumpers, and the field operators. I rode around in their trucks with them and went into the plant as they walked their rounds. At every step of the way I observed what they did, and I soaked in everything I could. This was an opportunity for me to learn what this business was at the ground level. I quickly came to appreciate what it takes to make this business work, day in and day out, and what we have to ask of our employees to see that the job gets done. I gained great appreciation and respect for the people who take on the many tasks that are required to operate safely, efficiently, and profitably.

For the rest of my career, whenever engineering sent out plans and project specs that detailed how we were going to do something this way, or to build it that way, I really had a hands-on appreciation for what I was asking them to do. I understood what they were being asked to do, and I understood what their limitations were. I also learned to go ask them first before jumping into a new project. They could keep you out of a lot of trouble if you just asked the right questions and listened carefully to their answers. My time at Katy was a truly invaluable experience. The fact that I had been sent there at the beginning of my career was no accident, of course. I believe it was by design, a conscious part of Exxon's management selection and training process. I may have believed at the time that my education had prepared me to spend my entire career as an engineer, but the truth was, engineering school was just the first step in what would quickly become a lifetime of leadership education. Exxon saw to that.

Exxon wasn't the first company to place management-track people in positions that would impart a broad understanding of what they might be dealing with in the future. That's the way Conrad Hilton did it with his family over the years—he made them work every position in the hotel before he would bring them into the management. I checked into a Hilton hotel in Houston once and got into the elevator. A polite young bellman had my bags. I looked at his nameplate and saw that it said, "C. Hilton IV."

"Your first name's not Conrad, is it?"

He shrugged and smiled. "Yeah. Great-Granddad said we've all got to start at the bottom." He explained that he was putting in a three-month stint working as a bellman and dealing with front door issues, which was a welcomed step up from the kitchen post he had just left. "Granddad always said, 'You can't run this place until you know what every one of your employees is doing.'"

My earliest posts with Exxon provided me with an array of comprehensive background experiences and an appreciation for the broad range of unique challenges that we faced as a company.

After Katy, I went to Tyler, Texas, where I did my first specialized work in subsurface engineering and became involved in developing hydraulic fracturing techniques. The process of hydraulic fracturing has become a public issue in recent years; but it has been around for a long time, and I personally have a long history with it. It was first tested back in the late 1940s. It really gained traction in the late 1970s and early 1980s, as we began to develop and improve fracturing techniques and other new technologies like horizontal drilling that would enable us to access previously inaccessible gas formations.

Tyler was right in the middle of it. I was based there for about 18 months, trying out different frack fluid formulations and different proppants, which were solid materials like man-made ceramic materials and treated sand. Today it's all sand, but early on we worked with alternatives, tried all kinds of things, different geometries, glass beads, sintered bauxite. Of course, we did all of this without the benefit of high-speed computers. My frack programs were recorded on punch card decks a foot long. I would run them at night on the computer at the office, and get page after page after page of printouts to tell me what I needed to know to tweak my designs.

After I had designed the jobs, I would go out to the well sites where they were to be run with the service companies that would be running them. We used three service companies at the time—Halliburton, the Western Company, and Baker Hughes—because none of them had perfected the process themselves. I had all three of those companies working for me, so I'd just about spend all my time on the road. I spent a lot of nights sleeping in the back seat of my car on well sites, getting ready for frack jobs.

It was a truly great way for me to start my career.

As 1977 came to a close I transferred to Houston, which was the Division office at the time. I was brought in as a production adviser, which was a technical adviser to the managers. I was able to provide practical feedback based on the knowledge I had gained from being in the field. I also worked on a lot of division-wide issues including corrosion control programs. All of these assignments broadened my perspective; it was another step in building an understanding of the vast and complex system that comprised Exxon.

My first supervisory assignment came in late 1979 as a gas facilities supervisor in Baytown. We had about a half-dozen natural gas plants there as well as some offshore production in Galveston Bay. It was while I was stationed there that I was faced with the tragedy of an on-the-job fatality for the first time in my career. An employee on one of the wells out in Galveston Bay had been killed, and I was named to lead the investigation into the accident. That entire experience made quite a powerful impression on me.

The district manager and I went to the man's home to tell his wife. He happened to have a brother who worked for us as well. He was a lease operator, a pumper. I had ridden around with those guys. I had then and have now great affection for them. It was a difficult thing to face. My job was to investigate what happened, operationally speaking and technically speaking, and to make sure that whatever might have gone wrong would never happen again. In doing so I found that his death was preventable. He had been checking a high-pressure gas well. Because of corrosion, the line parted with great force, knocking him unconscious, and throwing him into the water. The response team got to him quickly, but he had already drowned. As a result of my investigation we were able to determine that we had a number of wells out in the bay that were on the verge of failing. We understood why, and we knew what we needed to fix them.

I worked with the research company, and I wrote the report describing the fix that was needed.

That tragic experience drove home the levels of risk that we live with and deal with every day in this business in a very poignant and personal way. That perspective has helped to frame my view of my work, my perspective on the company and its relationships with employees, as well as the relationships we have with communities we operate within and other entities we work alongside.

Today, when I am asked any variation of the question, "So, what do you really do?" I reply that I am in the risk management business. That is the substance and essence of what I do—I manage risk.

I manage operational risk, financial risk, and political risk. I also manage environmental risk. When I travel around the world and speak with members of our organization, I always seek to empower them this way: "You're in the risk management business, too. You may be a field operator, process operator, engineer, or driller. You may be an admin back in the office. It doesn't matter what position you are in. In our risky business nothing can be taken for granted. You can never assume anything about conditions, equipment, or personnel. You can't automatically assume that people have done their job entirely or properly. It doesn't matter if you work behind a desk or if you've got callouses on your hands: you are in the risk management business, I tell everyone in the company, every one of you, whether you realize it or not. Bearing that responsibility is a part of your job, just like it is a part of mine. I am responsible, you are responsible, we are all—together—responsible."

The experience early in my career of losing someone that I knew had a profound effect on me. It changed me. I knew him personally, and I knew his brother. Dealing with that loss was personal. Today, whenever a person is killed on an ExxonMobil operation, I still take it personally, even if I didn't know him. That tragedy all those years ago marked a turning point for me. From that point forward, everything I do has been framed in terms of risk management. How can we always do what needs to be done—given that some of that will involve extraordinary risks to people and property—while still making sure that nobody loses his life? It's a tall order, but we have a pretty extraordinary record, given the exposures we have. Our mantra today is "Nobody gets hurt." That's not just a slogan. I tell people it's my belief that we can achieve that. As a corporation, we've never achieved it yet, but we have managed operations with hundreds of people who have gone years now where nobody's gotten hurt. I know it can be done. Logistically, it's a human behavior problem more than it is an engineering or facility problem.

My hope is that we can have a year where we have no fatalities. We have had years where there were no employee fatalities, but we have a large number of contractors who work for us all over the world, and we've yet to have a year of zero contractor fatalities. I hope we reach that goal soon, and that every year thereafter is a year with zero fatalities. We have a shared responsibility to do everything we possibly can to minimize exposures and protect people while still getting the job done.

5

To say that you can't be something you're not might seem obvious, but my experience tells me that this is a maxim that bears repeating. It is a truth that is universally applicable, but it is especially relevant to those who are operating in any kind of leadership role. I have certainly found it to be true over the course of my career. I see so many people in leadership positions try to emulate or copy the style of others, but it never, ever works. People see right through it. A leader must lead and work with his management team, on his terms, in his style. In short, a leader has got to do what works for *him*.

It takes a lot for a person to fully develop his or her leadership style; and development is a never-ending process. I believe a person is never finished developing because we are shaped by what happens to us and by the things we do. We are shaped by our experiences. As long as you are alive, every day you wake up and walk out into the world, life experiences await you. Those experiences may be significant or insignificant, profound or superficial, good, bad, ugly, or beautiful. Nonetheless, every experience is a formative experience. If you're not developing, you're not living.

A leader who attempts to copy the style or model that proved successful for another leader, in another setting, under different circumstances, won't develop his own unique style, including the skills that might make him most effective. Leadership isn't easy. So many factors must be balanced.

In part, it involves understanding followership, appreciating the nuances involved in working with peers, working with older peers, dealing with the unique issues associated with managing people that might be older or more experienced than you, and generally understanding how to empathize and relate to the people around you—different people, with different personalities and backgrounds, somewhat different values, different skills, different attitudes—some of whom you're naturally going to like quite a bit, and some of whom you might not be inclined to invite over for family dinner.

As I moved up to each new position of greater responsibility within the company, I learned that as important as the ongoing development of my idiosyncratic style of leadership was, there were also larger and larger considerations that I now had to grapple with related to questions and factors of institutional leadership. What, for instance, is an institution's style of leadership? Is there an ideal style of institutional leadership? How does an institution affect a change in leadership style? Can an individual affect a change in an institution's leadership style? If so, how? How do you, as a leader, approach developing the leaders who ultimately will be tasked with leading other leaders?

As CEO and chairman, I've had an entire stratum of corporate senior vice presidents reporting to me. Then there are presidents of all our companies under them. Beneath the presidents layer is yet another layer of vice presidents. In total, we currently have about 83,000 employees spread around the world. I do not, and I cannot, just worry about leading those who report directly to me. I have to lead all 83,000, from the senior VPs and presidents to the roughnecks on job sites. Now, I may not come into personal contact with roughnecks any longer, but I sure know they're watching me. I know they're looking, more so today than ever before. The internet and other tools of instant communication make sure of that.

A leader—like the institution he serves—cannot be complacent. If you ever think you have all of the answers and have achieved your development to its fullest potential, you're in trouble. You could only ever get to that conclusion if you're not paying attention. There is always room to grow. An important quality in every successful leader is a willingness to look in the mirror and be unafraid of whatever you might find. A leader must be honest with himself and continually practice and develop self-awareness.

I had to learn to recognize when something was making sense to me, but not making sense to the other people in the room. Clarity in communication is of the utmost importance. It is imperative that everybody in the room understands completely and without question what the position is, and that no one walks out with even a slightly different view or formulation of that in his mind. I have to constantly be asking myself: How did what I just said, or what I just did, get interpreted by the people who heard me say it or saw me do it? What did my body language communicate? What about my tone of voice? A successful leader consciously balances these factors and reduces the possibility for misinterpretation to a minimum.

I believe this ability is one of the factors that separates a person who is a good leader from a person who is a competent manager, or more broadly, distinguishes leadership from management hierarchically. You can be a proficient manager and not be a particularly good leader; but if you're a good leader, you ought to be able to be a good manager.

Management is something that can be learned; there is almost a formula to it. Leadership is something that is developed over time. I don't think there's a formula for leadership. There are certain attributes and behaviors associated with successful management and leadership that can be picked up intentionally, but the most important lessons are absorbed through experience.

The thing that sets some leaders apart from others, I think, is what they're able to do with what they've learned, based on their own life experiences and the depth of their own value system. The thing that separates the great leaders from the good leaders is conviction.

The leader of strong values and great conviction can face any situation unafraid. If you don't have questions in the back of your mind as to whether or not it is the right thing to do, because you know you are standing on your values, then you are free to act. If you know that what you are doing is the right thing to do, then you are almost decoupled from the outcome. It almost doesn't matter how it actually turns out. I believe that's what separates the great leaders from the good leaders—the depth of their conviction. Of course, you can have the most conviction of any person on this planet, but that doesn't mean you won't experience failure and disappointment. It does mean you will have a better chance of sleeping soundly at night.

It is your conviction that gives you the self-confidence to stand in front of people and talk and to motivate them. It has to come from inside of you. Somebody can write you a great speech, but if the words aren't yours, if the message isn't your own, it will fall flat. You don't have to have the largest vocabulary in the world or be the most articulate person—but you do need to be authentic.

The flip side of speaking with conviction is following through on the words you speak. Large companies and government bodies have armies of lawyers who generate thousands of pages of fine-print legal jargon when spelling out the details of complex agreements. But even the most complex deal begins with a few people sitting around a desk stating their positions and describing their objectives. When meetings like this, even informal ones, reach agreements in principle, it is critical that each person who makes representations about what role they are prepared to play in the developing deal is fully prepared to stand behind what they say. Your convictions shape your words. Your word is your bond. Together they comprise two of the most important characteristics of leadership.

When you as a leader are asking a person to undertake something that is very difficult or very personally challenging, it is your conviction that enables them to buy in and to follow you.

I hold certain beliefs to be inviolable. There are, I believe, certain things that are true no matter the circumstances, no matter the time, no matter the application. I'm not sure that I would be an effective leader if I didn't have that conviction. I can hold any vision, any projection, any goal or plan up against those values. That makes the business of sorting through what works and what doesn't work, at least in my view, pretty easy.

6

As a man tasked with significant responsibilities, I have often looked to the example of successful leaders. There are many leaders throughout history who possessed unimpeachable values and conviction with a force sufficient to motivate masses and accomplish exceptional feats. There are some that stick out in my mind more than others. Abraham Lincoln is one of those leaders.

I believe that Lincoln's personal integrity, his persistence, and his optimism in the face of horrendous conditions were truly remarkable. He was often faced with almost unimaginably difficult decisions. He had a deep set of principles and convictions that enabled him to make the hardest decisions anybody had to make. That is not to say that his principles and convictions were immutable. He went through an enormous personal evolution in his own views when he was writing the Emancipation Proclamation. He spent a long time writing and rewriting it. He went over, and over, and over. On complex issues he took enormous amounts of time to get where he needed to be, to be certain that he had all of the information and understanding he felt he needed to be properly and thoroughly informed. Once he arrived there, he didn't hesitate in making a final decision. That process sometimes took a while.

I find him to be a compelling figure and good example for a number of other reasons. The fact that he came from a very modest background, was completely self-educated, literally taught himself the law out of books—all of this points to an extraordinarily driven and persistent individual.

It is easy for us to lose sight of his personhood from the distance of a century and a half. He was lanky and a bit ungainly and had an eccentric beard. That is well-known. But most people don't know that his voice—this instrument that delivered some of the most hallowed words in human history—was in fact high-pitched and frequently referred to as annoying. He spoke in a twangy, backwoods drawl that lent itself more readily to an uneducated farmer, not the iconic figure who would be remembered as one of the most transformational leaders in the history of the world. But his words were powerful, and no one remembers the voice that delivered them. Lincoln was so careful with the words he selected. He was a meticulous communicator, one who placed a high value on clarity. He would labor over a word choice to make sure he had the one word that was right for the situation—so that when any person read or heard the word, there would be zero question as to what it meant and what he was saying.

I can appreciate how difficult it is to eliminate any possibility for misinterpretation. When you reach the point of doing that consistently, you have achieved the ultimate in building your unique leadership style. It involves harmony and clarity in verbal communication and non-verbal communication. In my view that definitely requires using the right vocabulary.

I have read some of Lincoln's personal papers, written in his own hand. I have seen where he changed words over and over, again and again, crossing one out and replacing it with another. He regularly agonized over the best choice of single words. It was almost as if that one word could change everything—and sometimes, it seemed that one word choice would lead to numerous other changes. I think that most people would look at those papers and see all of the word changes and think that any of the words he tried would have worked fine. But that's not how it was for Lincoln. He kept at it until he got exactly the right one, the word that would ensure no one could misunderstand what he was saying—the word that delivered the same meaning to everyone who heard it.

I was fortunate early in my career to have a boss who cared that much about language and communication. His name is Judd Miller Jr. He was the vice president of natural gas for Exxon Company USA around 1987, and I was his business development manager. Judd was one of the most deliberate communicators I ever worked with. He's been retired for many years now, but he is still a very close friend.

I often helped to write the speeches he gave to the management committee. At the time, writing those speeches was the most agonizing experience of my life. I would sit with him in his office with a draft of a speech I had worked on for him. He would take a pencil, cross out a word, and then bite the end of the pencil and sit absolutely still. He wouldn't move. He would just stare at the page for what seemed like hours, but was probably only three or four minutes—three or four really long minutes. Then he would finally write a new word down, and read the sentence out loud to get my reaction. That level of precision drove some people nutty. But he rarely would have to repeat something or correct himself or restate something for clarity.

I later worked for two other men who followed the same pattern of deliberate, word-by-word reflection. It turned out that they had all worked together. All were of the same vintage. At some point, somewhere in the past, some teacher or boss must have taught them to write that way. In any event, Judd's writing and editing process made quite an impression on me. It helped me to develop a heightened appreciation for how powerful clear communication could be. That is why I try to be deliberate in the way I communicate today.

That sequence mostly involves my mouth not getting ahead of my brain when I'm speaking. To accomplish that I have to speak at a fairly slow, measured pace, so that I have time to think about the words I'm choosing. I also check to see that the people I am addressing comprehend what I'm saying. I speak to large audiences on a regular basis. Sometimes when you are addressing a crowd of over 1,000 people in a large auditorium you have to deal with stage lights that make it difficult for you to gauge the responses of every individual in the audience the way you can do in a more intimate venue. But even in those larger group settings, I am constantly looking at the people that I can see to judge whether or not they appear to be getting what I am trying to communicate. I also learned that I could accomplish more with my communication if I varied the pace of my delivery. That gives people ample time to both hear and process what I am saying.

If I'm speaking in a situation where I know I have a specific time allotment and audience, I usually have written out what I want to say. But it's not unusual at all for me to do it right before I speak, and I may change words then, even though I've worked through it three or four times. Then as I'm delivering the speech it's not uncommon for me to not use the word change I just wrote down. Why? Because I am constantly getting cues from the responses on the faces of the people in the audience. Usually, as I come to those places in the speech, my mind naturally comes to exactly the right word. Experience and a lot of practice go a long way towards making those kind of mid-speech adjustments.

There is a lot of wisdom in the old KISS acronym: Keep It Simple, Stupid. Many people inject far too much complexity into their communications. I think sometimes that happens out of insecurity and the mistaken belief that if they toss around complex jargon and ideas they will be conveying the impression that what they have to say is especially important. (And, of course, that the messenger is important, too.) According to their logic, the more complex you make the communication, the smarter and more important you must be.

I've learned early on in my career that just the opposite is true. When I started out I felt the need to impress people. I wanted to let my bosses know that I knew what I was talking about. It wasn't long before I found myself injecting ever more complex words into the statements I was making. That's where paying attention gets real important: you see, when you notice the eyes of your audience glazing over, it's pretty clear you are doing something wrong. It became evident to me in no time that my complex-word strategy wasn't working, and I gave it up for good. Over the years I have tried to express myself with greater simplicity and clarity, and that includes when I'm talking to the most sophisticated of people, whether it's the president of the United States, or the Council on Foreign Relations, or university professors. I try to keep it simple.

Sometimes I will listen to one of my managers giving a presentation or coaching his team, and it becomes clear to me that he isn't doing the most effective job of making his point. I don't berate people in front of others; I have never found that to be effective. But I will call him up after the fact and say, "That presentation you were making was pretty confusing. Did you feel it was confusing as you were saying it?" Usually he will acknowledge that was the case. When I ask, "So, what is it you wanted to tell us?" At that point he will usually just blurt out the message clearly and directly.

"Well then, why didn't you just tell us that if that's what you wanted to tell us?"

"Well," he will say, "I felt like I had to set it up before I explained it, and then I needed to go into the details…"

I have found that most of the time, the simpler you make it, the higher the chance your message will be communicated to the audience successfully. After all, the goal is for everybody leaving the meeting to have comprehended the entire message. It doesn't matter whether everybody leaves the meeting thinking you are the smartest guy in the world. If you get everybody to understand the goal, the chances of success go way up. The more successful you are as a leader, the smarter you appear; you don't achieve more success because you appear smart.

I tend to shoot for the lowest common denominator when speaking to a group. I take the temperature of the room. I look around and see if people are following what I'm talking about. If people are having difficulty understanding what I'm trying to say, the onus is on me to adjust my delivery and reframe my message so that everyone does understand. And, if it so happens that the folks who did already get it are bored listening to me explain it again for the benefit of the people that didn't get it the first time through, that's okay. I'd rather have people be bored and understand the message than not understand the message and be enthused. My only objective in those situations is to ensure that everybody leaves with a common understanding.

Aim for the lowest common denominator. Keep it simple. Your message will get through.

7

I HAVE FOUND that when you are running an organization it is best to try to give as few directives as possible. You can't make every decision yourself. Nor can you personally direct each person into doing what he or she specifically needs to be doing. Even if you could, that wouldn't be the best usage of your time. Instead, what you can and should do is to make sure your team is properly aligned.

I used to teach at our management schools where I asked my managers to think in terms of a navigational compass. "You don't have to tell everybody, 'Okay, now we're going to go 271 degrees and 15 seconds.'" All you need to tell them is, "We're going northwest. We're not going northeast. We're not going southeast. We're not going east. We're going northwest." Achieving proper alignment involves simply getting everybody to face northwest.

As a leader if you do more than that, or less than that, you can get your entire team out of proper alignment. And that can lead to terrible results.

I used a diagram for that training that illustrates how a group is empowered. The chart shows the relationship between responsibility on one axis and freedom to act on the other. Where you have a high degree of freedom to act, but low responsibility, you get chaos. In other words, everybody can do whatever they want to do, but they're not responsible for the consequences, so you have utter chaos.

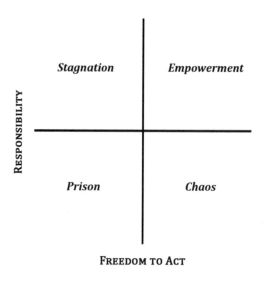

A situation in which you have a low degree of freedom to act and low responsibility might best be described as prison. You don't have any freedom, and somebody else is responsible for what you do.

When you have low freedom to act but high responsibility you get stagnation. Under those conditions you're holding people responsible for what happens but you're not giving them the freedom to direct what happens. Even if they see a problem, they don't have the power to do anything to fix it—they are helpless and still responsible for it when it goes wrong—that's unfair, and it leads to nothing but stagnation and frustration. Managers trying to work under those conditions tend to just stop looking for problems altogether.

When you have high freedom to act and high responsibility, you are empowered. That is the optimal working environment—a situation in which you have adequate freedom to act, and where you will be held accountable for your actions. When an entire group operates under those conditions, you have achieved organizational empowerment.

In the 1980s, American management theory became hyper-focused on the concept of empowerment. The idea took off like a rocket. The concept grew out of the system of continuous improvement, kaizen, which was the ethos and system of management that rebuilt Japan after WWII. Empowerment was the big catch word at the time, but it did get us thinking about which conditions would lead to an optimal work environment peopled by employees who cared about their jobs, took the initiative, and operated with high efficiency.

Up to that point, the Exxon that I knew might be described as a system of management by objectives. This management system frequently pushed us into periods of stagnation. Management would set certain objectives, and you were responsible for meeting them. So far so good. Oftentimes, however, you weren't provided with the means or support or authority you actually needed to get the job done. Over and over again, objectives were set and responsibilities were doled out, but the tools to meet the objectives were not delivered in the mix. The result was continued company stagnation. In all, Exxon spent about ten years in that spot. Looking back, one of the turning points in my career occurred when I was tasked with identifying and recommending a resolution to the problem.

I came up under the system of objectives-driven management that characterized Exxon. That trained me to work in a certain way. I got up every morning, went to work on time, and worked hard. The thought that I was eventually going to get fired idled constantly in the back of my mind. I never felt like I was doing well enough, and I was just so thankful to have a job. So I just worked hard, did the best I could, and never paid attention to the bulletin board where notices of promotions were posted.

In 1979 I received my first supervising opportunity. I was a facilities gas engineering supervisor in Baytown, Texas. Six engineers worked for me. In 1980 I was sent down to Kingsville, Texas, and became a district engineering manager. Kingsville was the second largest district of Exxon USA, and that was where I had my first large organizational management experiences. First I was a senior supervisor there, and I had about 35 or 40 engineers. Six months later, they moved my boss out, and they moved me up, and suddenly I had about 110 engineers working for me. That was one of the most exciting times of my life. The oil industry was going gangbusters. We had drilling rigs working all over the place, we were laying pipelines and building facilities, and I was just having a ball. I was working my tail off and loving every minute of it. I was 28 years old, I had 110 engineers working for me, and I had a $300 million annual budget.

Then I got transferred to headquarters in Houston to work on the planning and reorganization assignment. I was stationed in the production company strategic planning organization. The vice president of production at that time was Harry Longwell, the man who would become my lifelong mentor and one who had a lot to do with my ending up at the helm of ExxonMobil. Harry put together the task force for the purpose of taking a look at Exxon's organizational structure and attempting to identify where we were stuck and how we could improve.

I was the youngest person on the task force. The rest of the team was mostly made up of senior manager guys in their 40s and 50s. I was 30. My assumption was that I had been placed there to be the grunt, the guy that was going to do all the administrative work. But I did more than that; I was fascinated by organizational structure. I did a lot of historical research on how we ended up where we were, and why we were organized the way we were.

I worked closely with another, more senior member of the team. He was four or five levels above me, and would be my boss a couple of different times in the years ahead. He and I would stay up late at night in front of the chalkboard, drawing out our ideas and concepts. Though it wouldn't be articulated in these terms until later, that's when this concept of the relationship between responsibility and freedom to act that is in the diagram above came to me.

After all of that work we concluded that if we wanted to improve Exxon efficiencies and results, the company would have to get rid of the long-standing management-by-objectives process. Needless to say, that conclusion on our part generated major controversy. The first time we took it upstairs to the management committee, they more or less threw us out. I left that meeting thinking, "That's it, my career is over. I'm probably going to be fired next week." I thought I was done.

It was encouraging then when Harry came up to us and said, "Y'all are doing great. Don't give up."

Sure enough, in the end, the company adopted a modified version of what we recommended in 1985. We got the structure right. I think Harry wisely recognized that if we got the structure right, the powers that be wouldn't have any choice but to accept the recommendations. We would have to leave the old, inefficient ways behind us. Stagnation is an untenable long-term position for any company to remain in.

The decision to change the management-by-objectives system set us on the path to implementing a lot of the continuous improvement theory. That theory held that you could be successful only if you were able to empower your entire organization. You had to empower the guy on the assembly line to stop the line if he saw something wrong. Everybody is responsible for quality, everybody is responsible for results. Deteriorating quality is going to cost you in the end. You might turn out more widgets, but if you've got a 25 percent widget rejection rate, you're going in the Dumpster. At least that's how continuous improvement worked on factory floors.

The problem for Exxon is that we were not in an assembly line manufacturing business. That was the struggle. How were we going to talk to people about the concept that you have to take authority over your piece of the collective work? Whether you're an engineer, geoscientist, roughneck, refinery worker, or a technician in the field, you are a part of the same system. We realized that looking at our business in that context it was somewhat like an assembly line. That being the case, if there was anything going on in the system that was problematic, someone (a whole lot of someones, in fact) needed the authority to say, "Stop the presses. We've got to fix this." That's how empowerment works.

What the management team feared was that if we attempted to empower people, management would lose control and the entire organization could spiral out of control and end up in utter chaos. That was how and why the diagram above came into being. We used it first to talk among ourselves, and then we used it later to train everybody in the upstream Exxon organization.

Understandably, our plan was met in some corners with skepticism. Some people looked at the chart and didn't believe us when we said we were going to empower them to this degree. They'd say, "I'm not going to stop the presses. I'd get fired." In turn we explained to them that with that degree of freedom comes responsibility. When you say, "I'm going to stop the assembly line," then you take certain responsibility for the consequences of that. So you have to be certain that you really have to stop the assembly line, as opposed to just making someone aware of an issue. There are a lot of ways you can deal with a problem, and sometimes stopping the assembly line is what you have to do. If that is what needs to be done, do it, we said. That is empowerment in action.

Through the process of educating everyone in the organization about the continuous improvement system we were also inculcating systemic values, including a feeling of genuine responsibility and ownership. We were getting everybody at every level in the organization to buy in. To the senior managers who were fearful that we would end up in chaos, I said, "The way you fix that is to make sure everyone understands what they are responsible for when they make their decisions. But here is the other side of this bargain, one we also have to live up to. Your people won't get it right 100 percent of the time. That's guaranteed. But as we are in the process of trying to teach them how to calibrate, we could push the whole organization right back over into stagnation—or worse—if we start shooting the first four or five people who stop the presses when they maybe didn't need to be stopped.

You have to mean it when you say to the organization, "We trust you and we understand you're not going to get it 100 percent right. When you don't get it right, we are all going to sit down and talk about why you didn't, so we can all learn from it. That's how we will all get calibrated." Of course, there were plenty of times where you really did just want to shoot the guy; but the whole organization was watching, and it didn't matter who it was that got shot. The first time you shot somebody, everybody would immediately scurry from empowerment back over to stagnation, and we would be back to, "I'm not going to do anything; that way I won't get into any trouble." A leader means what he says. His word is his bond.

This was not an overnight transformation: It took about three years to educate everyone in the organization, five years before I really felt like people bought in, and ten years before we were really good at it. By that time, somewhere in the mid-1990s, it just became the way we worked. Today there are generations of people who have joined the ExxonMobil organization that never experienced the old management-by-objectives way.

Empowerment became central to how the entire organization operated. It applied all the way from how we talked about risk management, to how we protected people, how we protected each other, the public, the communities in which we operate, and the environment. You simply can't achieve those things if your people are not empowered. They are the ones who know what the risks are. They know where the problems are and they've got to have the authority to shut this thing down if they think that we've put people at risk, the public at risk, the environment at risk, or our reputation at risk. They have to know that we will always stand behind them if their reasons for doing it were consistent with our directives, our values, and what we've told them. Yes, we may have to help them calibrate from time to time. That's all part of the process.

We do a tremendous amount of what I call reappraisal at Exxon. We look back on every decision we take. It's amazing to me the number of companies that don't do that, or that merely look at the results of a given decision. We look at not just the result, but how we arrived at the result, and compare that result to what our expectation was, and we ask ourselves how we might have gotten an even better result or achieved the same successful result in a better way. There is a full reappraisal process we go through annually on all of our investment decisions. I call it the license to operate. When it comes to safety, security, health, and the environment, anytime we have to shut something down, or anytime we have an incident, the whole system gets reappraised, right then and there.

The conversation for the appraisal begins with, "You did the right thing. Let's take a look at everything that happened now, because we're going to learn from this, and you are helping us understand. What else could we have done? How might we prevent it from happening in the future or deal with it differently?" Then the people involved in the appraisal become part of the whole process of us all learning together, and they buy into it. At this point they really understand that this is part of our culture. It's how we do business. I experienced an appraisal situation myself, and the managers above me weren't critical. That made a huge difference in my own thinking whenever I was faced with a decision. I knew with absolute certainty that we now worked in a culture in which we talked openly about critical issues, learned from our mistakes, constantly learned from each other, and taught each other. That is only possible when every individual in the organization is empowered.

8

AFTER MY WORK WITH THE TASK FORCE I became a manager of business development in the Natural Gas Department. Among other assignments, I worked on the permitting side for the Alaska natural gas pipeline. That was a period when the United States deregulated natural gas pricing and unbundled natural gas transportation. All of our previous contracts—dating back for years—had been put together under the old regulations. The unbundling meant that we had to go back and restructure and renegotiate contracts, which was a tremendous amount of work.

It was a contentious and exciting show, and I had a front row seat. I traveled to Washington, D.C., frequently to work with the Federal Energy Regulatory Commission—the FERC—on the regulations. I also went to Ottowa, Canada, on a regular basis to work on the cross-border treaty transit agreements with the Canadian government to make way for the Alaska pipeline.

This was the first assignment in which I had to deal with federal governments up close and personal. It was a bit daunting to me as a young guy. I had dealt with local regulators before, but this wasn't anything like that. I had to learn how those processes worked, and develop a deep appreciation for the political side of the business. The work extended far beyond simply meeting what the prevailing regulations said. This entire experience was a crucial part of my development as a leader.

In this, as in other business (and political) settings, there will always be people who want to stop you. People come into negotiations with all kinds of perspectives: business, politics, the environment, and so on. You need to be very well-prepared, and that means doing your homework. You can't go into meetings and make mistakes, in part because everything that transpires in the conference room is on the record, including anything you say. You have got to make sure that everything you are telling people is correct. If you screw it up, your mistake is there for the world to see for all time.

One of the tenets of our management development system involves the constant measurement of how each manager is performing, combined with training as they move from job to job. We are, first, testing their capabilities to see how they deal with challenges. Then we develop their skills and their talents through the experience.

I'm not sure exactly when it was that I first recognized that I had come to the attention of senior management. Even after I had completed work on the organizational task force with Harry Longwell, I was initially just happy to have survived the experience. I developed a great relationship with Harry, and I could tell that he was supportive of my continuing development for leadership roles in the company. That support has continued to this day.

When I worked for Judd Miller Jr., I was also aware that it was something of a test job for me. I began to understand that if I continued to perform well, good things would happen. At the same time, I thought I had my ultimate potential pegged pretty well. My highest career goal was to be an Exxon division manager. If I could achieve that, I thought, I would have achieved everything I could possibly have hoped for in my career.

In 1989 I became general manager of Exxon USA's Central Production Division, which meant I was responsible for oil and gas production operations in parts of Texas, Oklahoma, Arkansas, and Kansas—one of the most highly visible posts within the company. I had been with the company for 15 years. I was 38 years old, and I had achieved everything that I had ever hoped to achieve in my career.

That was simultaneously a great and yet not-so-great circumstance to be in.

I know now, because I run the system, that my posting as general manager was one of those pass/fail jobs. You were either able to do it, or you couldn't. It was, in effect, a weeding out mechanism used by the company. Some people who had the job before and after I did succeeded; some failed. Failure didn't mean that they got fired. It just meant that their true potential for continuing development in the system was something different than what we had thought, and sometimes, even different than what they had believed.

In my own experience, I was so caught up in trying to just do the job of general manager that I didn't have any time to worry about failure. It was at this time that I was doing a lot of the work on theorizing how we could enact the theories of empowerment we believed could help to transform the company and end a period of prolonged stagnation. One of the men working for me at the time was really helpful because I could bounce ideas off him. He was very creative and he helped develop many of the concepts by which we could implement the empowerment ideas.

Still, I felt pretty overwhelmed because I was one of the youngest guys who had ever been put in a job with those responsibilities. Not only that, everybody who worked for me was older than I was. That presented all kinds of challenges.

But I was on top of the world. I had achieved my dream job and I was only 38 years old. If you had asked me at the time I would have told you that I would have done that job for the rest of my life and been completely content. Exxon, though, had other plans for me.

In 1992 I was sent to Dallas, Texas, to become a production adviser to the management committee and the board. Any investment proposal for $50 million or more goes to the management committee for review and approval. Anything that came from the producing side of the organization, which was where 85 percent of all the investment dollars were spent—offshore platforms, exploration wells, big offshore producing facilities in Africa, big jobs in Russia, or other places around the world—these proposals came into the management committee for their endorsement.

My job was to review those proposals and try to spot any gaps or problems or risks in them. Then I would write a cover memo for the management committee along the lines of: "Exxon Australia is proposing to set a platform in this location for $250 million. Here are the economics. I've looked at it. It makes sense. I support it for these reasons, but here are the areas of risk that I can foresee." Sometimes the conclusion of my review was, "I don't support this and here's why."

As time passed I was called into the offices of various members of the management team who would ask me to talk them through all of the aspects of a given proposal. I was also given some special studies by Chairman and CEO Larry Rawl.

One day out of the blue Larry sent me a simple note. It read: "Rex, why aren't we in China, Russia, or Mexico?" That's all it said. That was typical of the type of "white paper" questions I would get.

That time period was an incredible experience for me. I wrote white papers, I did research, and I advised. Then in 1994 the company sent me to New Jersey to be manager of international gas sales, which put me into a commercial job once again. At that time, Exxon was the largest marketer of natural gas in continental Europe. I had responsibility for our natural gas sales in Europe, South America, and Southeast Asia. I had to go where the business was, so I began to do a lot of global traveling.

As I started to get international exposure, I came to appreciate the nuances of dealing with different cultures and traditions than those I had grown up with. I sat down with a lot of ministers—oil ministers, finance ministers, economic ministers. I had butterflies at first. It was a new experience for me. I'd had a bit of an opportunity to travel in corporate, but only a couple of times. And those meetings weren't my meetings; I was just an observer. It is a very different feeling when you are heading into a meeting with a specific agenda that you yourself are responsible for accomplishing.

I spent less than a year on that international gas job. Six months after I started we ran into a big dispute in Yemen, the nation at the southern tip of the Arabian Peninsula.

Now, my boss's boss started each morning at 7:30 with a bagel and cream cheese and a cup of coffee at his desk. One morning he called me into his office, and, while eating his bagel, he shook his head and without looking up at me said, "I can't believe I'm going to do this." He laughed and looked up at me.

And then he dropped it: "Don't have a heart attack, but I need you to go to Yemen," he said. He went on to explain what the problem was. "This thing is a real mess. It's headed for the international courts. When it goes to the courts, the lawyers can take care of it and you can come back here. But I need you to get down there. It'll take six months, maximum."

Just like that, I flew off to become president of Exxon Yemen. At the same time I also became president of Esso Khorat, which was our Thailand upstream affiliate, because they were in the middle of a big gas contract renegotiation, as well. I made 17 trips to Yemen in that first 12 months, staying in the country for a week or two each time. It certainly seemed like I was spending more time there than back home.

I eventually got the Yemen situation sorted out and positioned to a place where going to arbitration was no longer necessary. It went so well that our partners in the deal installed me as lead negotiator, which led to two and a half years of one of the most complex negotiations I have ever been involved in. The end result was an agreement that was 917 pages long—plus 17 side letters. It was one of the most complicated deals we had ever undertaken, but we got it done and signed.

Before the ink had even dried on the deal, management called. They said, "You did a great job. Now, we need you to go to Russia."

9

IN 1998 I WAS NAMED VICE PRESIDENT OF EXXON VENTURES and president of Exxon Neftegas, and I was tasked with overseeing a complicated situation in a complicated corner of the world.

Sakhalin Island lies immediately off the east coast of Russia in the North Pacific Ocean, close off the north shore of Hokkaido, Japan. Throughout history the island has changed hands between Russia and Japan numerous times. Some of the native people on the island identify with Russia, and some identify with Japan. At the end of WWII, Russia took control of the island from Japan, and has held it ever since.

It had long been thought that there might be large oil reserves off the island. Until the dissolution of the Soviet Union, though, there wasn't a way for outsiders to participate in that potential business. As we began to get involved it was clear that there were enormous logistical and political difficulties we would need to handle in order for the effort to prove worthwhile. We had signed one of only two production sharing agreements in Russia to operate offshore of Sakhalin Island. At the time I was assigned to the situation there were a number of government agencies and representatives that were either directly involved or trying to become involved after they understood that our investments could prove to be very profitable. There were also some questions as to which claims held primacy and we were dealing with a conflict with the governor of Sakhalin at the time that I took over that operation.

A big part of the challenge is the location. The meta-ocean conditions offshore Sakhalin are among the most severe in the world. They're much worse than Alaska, for instance, because it's sheet ice that fills in, not pack ice or icebergs. The water is shallow, and so these giant sheets, almost like tectonic plates, rift upon themselves with all the force of nature, as if they're being pushed by the biggest locomotive in the world. This relentless force just keeps pushing and pushing these gargantuan sheets of ice. It's a sight to behold. It gouges huge trenches in the ocean floor. It will crush or push absolutely anything out of its way. That meant that any sort of conventional offshore facility was impossible.

Generally, the ice will retreat enough by July 1 that you have open water. That allows you to work with conventional equipment for a few months, but you have to be out of there by October 1, because at that point the fall storms set in. These storms are almost like mini-hurricanes. They generate these massive waves that come rolling in shallow water, much like a tsunami—waves that can destroy anything manmade. Then it gets cold again, and here comes the ice.

On top of the cold and the storms and the waves and the ice, the area is also one of the most seismically active locations on the planet. They have a lot of earthquakes—some of them quite massive. The year before I arrived an earthquake killed 3,500 people.

It's also a very sensitive environment. The region is home to one of the feeding areas that the North Pacific gray whale uses during its calving season. They feed right in the area where we are trying to operate. They are an endangered species with only about 130 of them in existence. Everything we do in the region incorporates protections for the whales.

For all of these reasons we designed and built the first ever shore-based drilling facility. It was the only solution that could address all of these complications. From mainland Russia, the facility drills out horizontally for over seven miles under the ocean, which allows it to avoid the treacherous conditions on the surface.

We were doing all of this in Russia, which at the time was a brand new country. In fact, when we signed the agreements Russia didn't really have laws or even a constitution. The communist system had been thrown out, but it still wasn't clear what kind of system would replace it. Various national and local bodies were trying to write laws and establish authority. Quite often those laws conflicted. Their regulatory agencies—their equivalents to our EPA, Department of the Interior, or Department of Energy—were struggling with new laws and regulations.

You would be hard-pressed to concoct a trickier set of circumstances under which to attempt a project of that scale. It is probably fair to say that it was no less challenging than successfully making the journey to Mars. The integration of technologies that were required to be accomplished are beyond most people's scope of imagination. We accomplished things in the process there that have never been done anywhere else in the world. The results, from a technical and engineering perspective, have been unbelievable. In the years since the first Sakhalin-1 well was drilled, a number of world record-setting wells for depth, rate of penetration, and directional drilling have been set there. The skill and drive of our people who accomplished these tasks amazes me year in and year out.

The economic results have been good, too. The project has been up and running for several years, and we have made significant profits for our shareholders, partners, and the Russian government.

We were faced with a unique combination of complex technical problems and relationship problems on Sakhalin. No one really thought it could be done. In the end, however, we were able to make it happen. To this day

Sakhalin is one of my proudest achievements.

As monumental and historic (not to mention complicated) as our operations on Sakhalin were, other events transpiring at the same time were noteworthy as well: Right when we were in the thick of things on Sakhalin, Exxon and Mobil were working through the largest and most high-profile corporate merger in history.

10

As the Exxon-Mobil merger was moving through months of regulatory approvals, a complete reorganization of the corporation took place. I had no part in that process, however. We were at a critical stage in our operations in Russia, and I was needed there to see it through.

Then, in December of 1999, just before the merger became official, I was named the executive vice president of ExxonMobil Development Company. The Development Company manages all of the major capital projects for the upstream side of the business. That is where the bulk of our capital spending occurs. If we've got to build an offshore platform in deep water, and we have to drill all the wells, or we're going to build a big LNG (liquefied natural gas) facility in the Middle East or in Russia, all of those kinds of projects are under the purview and responsibility of the Development Company. Potential projects come to fruition only after the Development Company conducts multiple rounds of engineering designs and feasibility studies. Once that was done we would run screening economics to see whether it made sense for us to invest in it or not. These projects take up to ten years to fully develop—they are very long time lines.

At the time of the merger, I went into the Development Company job and the first task at hand was go to through the inventory of all of the project opportunities that Exxon had, and all of the project opportunities that Mobil had at the time. We had to gain an in-depth understanding about where the Mobil projects stood in terms of the legal agreements that were in place with governments that controlled those potential investment opportunities. What were our relationships like in those countries? What were are all the risks? Which opportunities were the most attractive? What were the timelines involved? How long would it take us to get any one of the opportunities in motion? I spent my first several months after the merger investigating these kinds of questions.

I traveled all over the world. I visited every single location where Mobil had a potential project in place and spent time getting to know the governments, getting to know the organization and infrastructure that was already in place on the ground in those countries, if any. We had to understand the capabilities of our people. Did we already have the right resources in place in terms of personnel and influence, or would we have to supplement what was in place?

That first year was a very intense and fascinating period. Just trying to sort out what we now had on our plate was a knotty undertaking. Then, too, we were doing this work in the midst of a number of enormous projects that were already well underway. For example, we were setting what at the time was the deepest deep-water facility in the Gulf of Mexico. It is called the Hoover-Diana platform, and it was nearing completion at the time of the merger. This platform floats vertically and is almost one-half a football field in diameter and 83 stories tall with drilling and production facilities installed. A production facility like this is designed to handle up to 100,000 barrels per day of crude and 325 million cubic feet per day of gas.

We formally launched Hoover-Diana at the end of the first year of the merger. That meant we were still working away on several complicated, world-class projects, while at the same time we were also trying to assess everything we now had in the combined Exxon-Mobil portfolio, to understand the people, and to put in place a set of processes so we could properly manage the risk and move the opportunities along.

We began to put organizations on the ground around the world that could deal with the host governments, the technical issues, and the political issues. Meanwhile, back in Houston, we got our project teams going on doing what they do so well, which is dealing with the technical aspects, the engineering, and the geoscience of the potential projects. Sometimes we were presented with a problem for which current technology offered a solution. In other instances where existing technology would not do the job we actually developed brand-new technologies so that we could keep moving forward. We would say to our teams, "Nobody has ever done this before, but you've got to go figure out how to make it happen." And that's exactly what they would do.

It was a fascinating and exciting time for the company, and for me professionally. There were a huge number of projects to tackle around the globe—about $50 billion worth of business. Obviously, you can't do $50 billion worth of projects all at once. We put together a system to allow us to prioritize potential projects, and to put them in a sequence that made sense. That included figuring out how to best deploy our people, our expertise, and our dollars.

Some of the projects did not make economic sense as they were configured at the time. So, we went back to the drawing board to figure out how to make them viable. In some cases we either had to have technology breakthroughs, or I had to go back and renegotiate the deal with the host government. I would tell them, "We just can't invest. You're going to have to work with us on this. You're going to have to change the taxes. We have to do something, because we can't do this project right now under these terms. If you decide you can work with us on these issues you know we're the best people to do the project."

I spent a lot of time on the ground meeting with government officials, helping them understand why their project was or was not moving forward. The system developed allowed us to prioritize these assessments, and every year we updated it. We were able to work through dozens of projects that way. You had to know what to work on, or what you wanted the organization working on each day. What was most important? What could you defer? How would you do that?

I had to travel to Dallas, Texas, to get each project approved, because they were multibillion-dollar deals. Through that process I got a lot of exposure to the Exxon executives there. After two years, I was visited in Houston one day by Lee Raymond, who was the chairman and CEO at the time.

"I want to talk," he said, "for the next 30 minutes. You don't need to say anything. Just listen. When I get done, if you've got questions, you can ask them." He told me he wanted me to come to Dallas to be on the management committee, and he explained his reasoning. There wasn't a whole heck of a lot for me to say. I relocated to Dallas in August of 2001, and became a senior vice president of ExxonMobil Corporation.

I was originally from the upstream side of the business. Another fellow was elevated from the downstream chemicals business at the same time. There were already senior VPs of upstream and downstream in place. The upstream senior VP was my old mentor Harry Longwell.

It was good that someone I knew well like Harry was around, because my new position sometimes presented me with challenges that I hadn't really faced before. The guy that I worked for before I moved up to Dallas was the president of the Development Company. He was my boss, and I answered to him. When I moved up to Dallas and joined the management committee I became his boss, just like that. Now he reported to me. There's no way to prepare yourself for that sort of 24-hour turnaround.

The truth is, I never recognized at the time what was going on in the larger scheme of things relative to my current or future role with the company. Some may find that hard to believe, but it's true. I thought I was coming in to replace Harry because he was going to retire in a few years. That's all I was focused on. I was completely consumed with the task of learning as much from him as I could so that when I took over his spot I could hit the ground running. I had learned a lot growing up on the upstream side of things, but there was an awful lot of the business beyond that I didn't know very much about at all. When I first moved to Dallas, I wasn't even thinking about Lee, or his job as chairman and CEO. It just never occurred to me.

I suppose that mindset is emblematic of my whole career. I was never a bulletin board watcher. When other people got promoted, I never related their promotion to my situation. I just went about my business. My whole career was spent trying to do the best job I could possibly do, no matter the job at hand. So, whenever the company moved me or promoted me, I was invariably kind of shocked. I invariably felt like I hadn't learned everything I was supposed to learn in the last job. They just kept moving me along so fast, I was always saying, "Man, I wish I could have stayed on in that position for another year. There's so much I could have done." But, they were already moving me on to the next job. Maybe it was the pace of it all that stopped me from paying attention to what was happening to the people around me—I wasn't in any one post long enough to get transfixed on which of my colleagues were or were not making big jumps. Even as I got to more senior positions, I rarely paid any attention or thought, "Gee, so-and-so just got named president of this company, and I didn't." My mind just didn't—and doesn't—work like that. I was so loaded up with the things they gave me to do, and so intent on making sure I did them well, that I just didn't have time to think about that kind of stuff.

After Lee Raymond told me to come up to Dallas, my current boss in Houston, the president of the Development Company—whose boss I was about to become—made a prescient comment that didn't resonate at all at the time. "Well," he said, "You snatched the gold ring." I thought he just meant that because I was going to Dallas.

"I told you that you were going to be chairman one day," he would later tell me.

"No you didn't," I said.

"Well, what did you think I meant when I said you'd snatched the gold ring?"

It really had never occurred to me that I was in line to become the head of what today is the largest company in the world. But that changed when Lee told me the board had decided they wanted me to replace him. I was the most shocked person in the world. I was genuinely stunned. I didn't see it coming, wasn't even thinking about it. In hindsight I should have seen it coming. But I was too busy trying to do the job they were asking me to do. Nothing has ever come easy for me. I've always had to work really hard. I've always known that I'm not the smartest guy in the room. I have always been busy working my tail off trying to be sure I'm doing a good job for these people that have entrusted me with immense responsibilities. I never had much time to sit around and think about it. Harry was another guy that didn't sit around worrying about anybody else. We were both so busy. Harry, I'm sure, knew. But, again, it's not like we ever talked about it.

Lee called me into his office and told me that the board had decided that I was the guy that would replace him when he retired. First I would be elevated to president of the corporation. That would give me a couple of years to learn about all of the things I had never been exposed to, so that I would be ready when he retired.

As I walked out of his office I was in a daze. I was absolutely stunned. It was a lot to take in. Frankly, it was kind of scary. I realized the enormity of it. Of course, my wife was very supportive. She always had a lot of confidence in me. She told me I could do it. My mother's voice echoed in my head: "Just do the best job you can do." That was all I could do, so that's what I set out to do.

On March 1, 2004, I was formally elected president of the corporation and a member of the board of directors. I moved down the hall to the corner office next to the boardroom by Lee's. I spent the next two years trying to just take in as much as I could about the things I felt like I didn't know enough—or anything at all—about.

The two years I spent as president of the corporation were very important for me. I developed a much deeper appreciation for and much more of an understanding of the enormity of this entity known as the ExxonMobil Corporation. I also came to appreciate, in ways I couldn't possibly have fathomed before, the significance and the importance of what we do through and for so many countries around the world: in so many instances, because we are there, they are better off. Our primary concern and mission is to be successful for our shareholders. Beyond that, we also feel an abiding sense of responsibility to share our values with the people we do business with around the world.

That's one of the messages I try to impart to policymakers in Washington who sometimes are critical of us. I go to some of these emerging countries around the world—whether it's Russia, or African countries, or Southeast Asian countries—and I take the American way of doing business with me. Even when their laws don't allow us to be as innovative or efficient or successful as we'd like to be, they get exposed to our way of doing things. These are our values. These are the business standards we operate by: honesty, integrity, and transparency.

There have been many times when those values have been put to the test in some of these countries. Other people and governments don't always conduct business according to our set of values. There have been times where we have had to say, "No. We don't do things that way, and we won't ever.

If you're saying that's what we have to do to do business here, then we just won't be able to do business in your country." We will not compromise on that principle.

In those two years I learned just how important those aspects of the corporation's mission were. Yes, we have got to invest well, and we must maximize efficiencies. We also have to generate long-term shareholder value. But in the 130-year history of this corporation, we have also had a significant influence on a lot of countries in terms of how they think and do things because we have stayed true to our values. That has had an impact on them, and I have seen and experienced that impact firsthand in the countries that I visit. The way we do business has caused them to change the way they do business. That is a legacy we are proud of.

It is a legacy I have done my best to forward since I took over as chairman and CEO of ExxonMobil on January 1, 2006.

11

IT IS DIFFICULT TO SEPARATE the values and business standards that we hold ourselves to from the free market system that produced them.

One principle people often forget is that failing in the free market system is just as important as succeeding. Failure imparts lessons that allow the best ideas and the best approaches to come to the fore. Failure actually supports innovation and spurs the innate creativity that exists in almost every person.

At its best a free market system, not governments or government policies, picks winners and losers. Ideally, a free market provides freedom for people to succeed and to fail. It creates a set of conditions that encourage people to put their beliefs to the test. Those who are willing to risk their capital to promote and realize their ideas can be handsomely rewarded. They can also go bankrupt.

Society has a tendency to recognize better ideas—"this is something I like, this is something I want"—and embrace them with purchasing power or political power. A good idea will flourish until something better comes along to replace it, at which point, if it doesn't continue to innovate, it will fail. But that's okay. Failure is a critical part of a healthy free market, free enterprise system. Bad ideas must be discarded so they can be replaced with good ideas, then good ideas are discarded in favor of great ideas, and great ideas are discarded in favor exceptional ideas, and so on.

Improvement means replacement, in part if not in whole.

In those countries that do not have a free market system, where everything is controlled by a central government—prices, investment levels—and the box is drawn very tightly around what you're allowed to do and not allowed to do, creativity and innovation tend to be greatly constrained.

I believe we are seeing some signs of this in the United States as well. That's why we are beginning to feel the increasing pressures of global competitiveness: Our government has involved itself in selecting what it thinks are the right answers on our behalf. I see the same thing in other governments around the world. All too frequently that approach means that innovation will be stifled and suppressed. Under such conditions, the person that has the best idea is actually at a disadvantage, because the government has already selected the idea they prefer.

In such circumstances the old ideas that have already been used and tested over and over again simply get recycled. The prevailing thinking among those who do this is that these solutions are safer because they are known. In practice, people, institutions, and governments that promote such recycling at the expense of genuine innovation are always going to be behind, and they are always going to operate at a higher cost, because, generally, these old ideas are less efficient. This begets inefficient use of capital, which begets inefficient development of labor, both of which point directly to lack of intellectual development, which occurs when governments intentionally or unintentionally define boundaries for economic performance and entrepreneurism and innovation. The end result is a society whose growth has been retarded, one that is operating at a lower level relative to other societies. In turn this attitude renders that society less competitive with the rest of the world. In my experience, the more governments intervene, the more they wind up holding their own society back.

Of course, there have to be some rules. No one is in favor of no-holds-barred no-rules-apply market conditions. That would be chaos. One of the chief reasons why the United States has been so enormously successful as an economic power in the world for the last 150 years is that there is a set of rules that clearly says, "Here's how we agree we're all going to govern ourselves." Those rules have to do with fundamental values including honesty, truthfulness, and fair play. A free market functions optimally when the playing field has been opened up to everyone, and all the government does is say, "Well, here are the laws and the rules. Follow them. Other than that, we're going to leave you be. Y'all figure it out."

When we talk about the market, people tend to think about it as this faceless entity. Well, it's not. It's 300 million Americans. They're the market, and they decide. They decide every day when they go to the store. They decide every day when they go online or pick up the phone to buy something or subscribe to a service of some kind. That is the system through which we promote the best ideas that America has to offer and discard the old ones that are no longer as valuable. The old ways and ideas may have been around a long time, but they have been overtaken by something else that we need. The sooner we discard the old ideas—or, the sooner that we stop protecting them—the sooner we'll advance to the next evolution in great ideas.

Innovation is what made our country an economic powerhouse. Unfortunately, we seem to be creating more and more confining boxes within our economy, and that stifles innovation. Some people seem to be almost ideologically opposed to innovation. Change can be difficult and unsettling; there is no question about that. If you as an individual or entity do not want to change, that's fine—just don't stand in the way of the rest of us who want to keep moving forward.

When it comes to dealing with change, fear is a base but powerful motivator. Today more than ever, the manufacturers of fear are standing in the way of the evolution and growth of great new ideas. Within the energy business, in particular, they are even standing in the way of open discussion.

When a leader is trying to sort out important policy matters they have to deal with the facts on hand. If you have hypotheses, or theories, or have areas that are unknown, you should identify and define them. Then, be prepared to examine those unknowns with the best knowledge available. In the energy business, that knowledge is scientifically based. As scientists and engineers, we know how to investigate and evaluate things that we don't fully understand so that we can make informed policy decisions.

If you have an environmental concern, if you are worried about our air or ground water being polluted, for example, these are understandable concerns to examine. To the extent that we may or may not be faced with problems in these or other areas, they are eminently solvable problems. These are issues for which there exist—or for which there can exist—scientific and engineering solutions. My position is that in these cases we should go and get those answers and develop those solutions.

But the manufacturers of fear don't really want answers based upon sound, objective examination to be presented in response to the fears they raise. That's because once we do have answers, the power of the fear-merchants will be diminished to the point of irrelevancy. When we invite the naysayers to join us in open, honest, fact-based conversation, we are almost always turned down. As a responsible business with a significant impact in the world in which we operate, we not only want to pursue answers, we must pursue them if we are to grow, innovate, and prosper. A fully and honestly informed public benefits from that perspective every bit as much as our company does.

If something to do with our operations anywhere in the world is thought to present a legitimate threat to public safety, we want to know about it immediately. We have every incentive in the world to fix any issue that might crop up. Most issues that occur can be fixed with good engineering and good science. It will come at a cost, but our response will be, "Here's how we can fix it, here's what it's going to cost us," or "Here's what that's going to mean for the cost to society for their energy." We can then sit down with policymakers and have a productive discussion based upon the facts: Is the cost worth it to the public and our shareholders, or not? If we as the stakeholders in our shared energy future (including the regulatory agencies and the public at large) don't like the costs that a given proposed change or new initiative might require, then we need to ask ourselves where our next source of energy will come from, and what's that going to cost.

We need to have these discussions. It is in the best interest of every concerned person and group to stop dealing with one another on this plane of fear when it comes to energy issues. We can and should approach these topics rationally: Here is what we know; here is what we don't know. With that data in hand we can construct a plan to go and find out more about what we don't know. To do all of this simply requires a willingness on the part of all concerned to hold the conversation.

Sadly, the energy sector is not the only place where fear often dominates the conversation in place of fact and the recognition of shared mutual interests. There are also those who manufacture fear in foreign policy, trade policy, and economic policy because doing so serves some narrow interest or ideology of their own. Many people choose not to deal with the facts; instead they traffic in wild speculation, hyperbole, and anxiety. Yes, I appreciate that there are few things in this world about which you can be 100 percent certain. But we can certainly apply our efforts to understand any situation better—no matter how complex or divisive it may seem. With better understanding we can confine the elements that are not knowable, or that simply we don't know at the moment, and start our work together right there. That is exactly how our thought processes work at ExxonMobil. We say, "Okay. That's the risk we have to go manage.

Do we feel comfortable with that risk or not?"

We are in the risk management business. We evaluate the technical attributes, the economics, the geopolitical risk, and the environmental risk. A lot of that we can define pretty well. But there are always pieces that we can't define. We recognize we have to take risk, but we believe in only taking risks that are manageable. The accuracy with which we make those determinations dictates our success. With every risk we manage, we learn things. Sometimes that risk wasn't as great as we thought it was. In the future then, we will recalibrate our risk management models to accommodate what we learned.

There's certainly nothing mysterious or new about this dynamic. This is the way society works. It's the way that the United States has operated for most of its existence. We have succeeded because individuals are willing to take risks, because society at large has been willing to allow individuals to take risks, and we have even been willing to take risks as a united people for the good of all society. Because we have taken risks, we have done extremely well. We have thrived. We have all but eradicated poverty, as most of the world defines poverty. Grinding poverty of the kind that afflicts so many millions around the globe doesn't exist in this country. We were able to end poverty here only because we were willing to acknowledge and accept risk.

Today we have arrived at a place where the manufacturers of fear have all but made it impossible for policymakers to acknowledge and accept risk. Europe arrived at that place about 30 or 40 years ago as they began to accept what is known as ruling by the precautionary principle. That principle says, "You have to prove to me there's no risk here. You have to prove to me that this isn't going to make me sick." The reasonable response to a challenge like that, of course, is something like, "Here is all of the scientific evidence; here's everything we know about the chemistry; here's everything we know about the epidemiology; based on everything we know, the risks are either not evident to us, or they're so low that we can't measure them." In the face of fact and reason, however, the purveyors of fear do not back down. Instead of examining the facts in the course of a healthy conversation, they are more likely to reply, "No, you must absolutely and conclusively prove that there will be zero risk, or we will not permit you to undertake the activity."

If you subscribed to the precautionary principle in your personal life you would never get in your car again because you can't prove that somebody else won't cause an accident and kill you. If you want to make sure you're never going to die in an automobile, under the precautionary principle, you would never get in an automobile again because you could never guarantee that you wouldn't get killed in a crash. Of course, we all drive around in automobiles every day, because we accept the fact that, yes, there is a risk, but I can live with that risk because of all the benefits I get from the mobility that my car provides.

That same rational thought process has to extend to things like hydraulic fracturing, or the development of new products with chemical processes. Once we get to the point where we believe the risk to be manageable, we move forward, continuing to monitor as we go, stopping if the information tells us otherwise. But the manufacturers of fear want us to live by the precautionary principle. "Prove to me it's not going to contaminate the groundwater, and then I'll tell you it's okay to hydraulically fracture." Well, we've got a million wells out there that are fractured, and so far we don't have a single documented case of groundwater contamination caused by fracking. "Not good enough," they say.

At some point, because of the enormous benefits that the product provides to society, society says, "We'll take that bargain," or "I'll drive my car." That's how economies flourish, people's quality of life improves, and we get ready to move on to the next important thing.

12

WHEN YOU ARE THE NEW FACE IN A HIGH-PROFILE POSITION, people will be curious about you. When I became chairman and CEO of ExxonMobil at the start of 2006, I recognized that curiosity presented an opportunity—at least for a while. People would pay a lot of attention to what I was saying at first, not because they thought I was smart, but because they were curious. Whatever I said, whether I repeated verbatim what had been said for years, or said something entirely new, my remarks would be construed as a major policy revelation. In short, people would be listening to me very carefully.

When I made the speech at the Wilson Center in 2006 in which I mentioned my views on climate change, I wasn't expressing an idea or position that was new. Far from it. We had been saying it internally within the company, and ExxonMobil had also been expressing it publicly for a few years by the time I gave the speech. Climate change was happening, and something would have to be done about it. Despite that, the media and others preferred to portray us as the poster child of climate change deniers. That wasn't true, but it was the narrative that had been woven over a long period of time. A major objective of mine in making that speech was to try to knock that perception out of the conversation—it wasn't just inaccurate, it was unproductive. Still, if people had been unwilling to acknowledge the stance we had been holding for years because it didn't fit their narrative about us, I was happy to take this opportunity to provide them with what they thought was a new narrative, even if it wasn't actually new.

It is critically important that we as a nation make informed decisions when it comes to energy policy. In the case of climate change, the press picked up and focused on what I said, when, in fact, ExxonMobil's position on climate change was not new. Climate change is a serious risk to society, one that needs to be managed like any other risk that we face. Period.

We need as a nation to acknowledge what we know and then begin by doing the things we know we can do, and by taking the actions that make the most sense. That's why we as a company advocate energy efficiency in every aspect of what we do. Advocating energy efficiency is certainly the easiest starting point for a serious campaign to deal with climate change. Every person can find ways to improve his energy use. There is a lot of capacity for energy efficiency in the system that consumers don't even know about, or that is not available to them. They should have that information. We must also continue to conduct first-rate climate science studies. Climate science involves arguably the most difficult and complex series of scientific investigations that are currently being undertaken by scientists in the world today. Sadly, the general public is woefully uninformed about the details of climate science.

In addition to acknowledging what we do know, we must also acknowledge what we don't know. We know that our climate is changing, but how exactly do we define that? What portion of that change is directly attributable to human activity? What portion is due to factors beyond our control? What are the short-, mid-, and long-term ramifications? How do we manage this risk in the future? These are questions for comprehensive and rigorous scientific and economic study and review, the results of which will call for us as a society to make some very tough choices.

Some organizations and individuals advocate for radical cuts of our carbon dioxide emissions to levels that nobody even knows how to achieve. When I speak to people who propose such action I ask, "What if we can't make those cuts? What if it is physically not possible? What if it is economically not feasible? What is your plan B?" Their typical responses to those questions include their refusal to accept that there are some questions that science cannot answer, and an equally adamant refusal to accept that there are some things that even the most spendthrift government cannot afford.

As a matter of personal and institutional policy, my principles have always dictated that we deal exclusively with facts. To do so means acknowledging equally what we know and what we do not know. I don't have any problem with admitting when I don't know something. Climate change is one of those areas. I cannot and will not ever claim to know more about something than I do, or make a statement that I cannot back up with analysis. If you as an individual or organization are willing to agree that we do not yet have all of the answers, and if in light of that acknowledgment you would like to proffer your prediction given that limitation, then by all means proceed. If we both agree that we don't totally understand this, you may view it one way, I may view it another, and that's fine; we are both interested in pursuing the truth, whatever it may turn out to be. To my way of thinking, that is the credible way in which to approach this situation.

Credibility matters, always, especially when you are in a leadership position. A big factor in being credible to those you serve is the extent to which you are consistent. That means showing up the same way, every time, no matter the situation. When I came into office, oil prices were trending up. When oil prices rise, the bull's-eye on our back gets even bigger. Most people aren't aware that companies like ours don't control the cost of oil. There are a whole host of factors involved when prices go up, from production and distribution issues to host country costs, taxes, political instability, natural disasters, futures market trends, and more.

In the early months of my tenure, costs were going up and up, and so we had to carefully watch capital formation and financing structures. What goes up, of course, almost always comes down. At some point prices correct. The financial crisis of 2008 saw a lot of business activity come to a crashing halt. As a leader, I needed to respond consistently to the realities of the circumstances around me, and that is equally true for good times as for the not-so-good times.

The same need for consistent leadership applies to the geopolitical arena. In my time at the helm of Exxon I have been faced with China continuing to evolve, the turmoil of the Arab Spring, Russia going through its own leadership transition, and major developments in Southeast Asia—quite a lot can happen in the span of a few short years. I don't know that my experience has been all that different from what my predecessors dealt with, though it does seem as if things have progressed with a bit more rapidity and drama than they did in the past. Any way you slice it, there has been a lot to deal with here at home and abroad.

I also recognize that when you are the chairman and CEO of the world's largest corporation, your voice registers louder and carries farther than most. It's an interesting experience when you recognize for the first time that the words you speak in public can cause the stock market to react. The awareness of the impact your words may have is another reason that credibility and consistency are so very important for a leader and his organization. I have sent other people on the management committee out to give speeches in which they publically articulate company positions and express the ideas, ideals, and standards of business conduct that we promote and advocate. The difference is, when I say the same things, the remarks tend to get picked up by the media. That is one reason I have not done a lot of public speaking. (Time is another reason. There is never enough of it.) One of the perks of leadership is having the luxury of picking and choosing where you want to speak and to which groups. I have tended to speak when there is something I want to say, a point I want to make, or a theme I want to introduce or emphasize in the public dialog.

A big part of the position I have occupied is participating in how public policy is formulated and decided. That's one of the things I learned during my two-year stint as president of the corporation: As CEO, I have a responsibility to talk about what, in our view, leads to success for all of us, for all of society, not just for ExxonMobil. If economies don't succeed, we don't succeed—we do poorly. When we have good economies, good economic growth, and prosperity reigns, we do well. That's when we create the greatest value for our shareholders. So I have spent a great deal of my time on economic, trade, and energy policy issues, and even on foreign policy issues in a quieter way.

When it comes to foreign policy, I have worked behind the scenes. It is not my role to get on the public stage and share my views, but I do try to inform the people who are trying to make those decisions, because I have had the opportunity to get to know many world leaders better than the policy makers know them. I say that with all due humility; one of the benefits of my position—another thing that is often overlooked—is that by the end of my tenure I will have served longer than most U.S. presidents spend in the Oval Office. In many cases I was dealing with some of these heads of state before they rose to their leadership positions. I have spent a lot of time in their countries and a lot of time with them personally. The result of the relationships I have built is that there are unique insights into these leaders that I can offer to policymakers for their use if they wish. When I see misunderstandings between various foreign officials, if I think I can help, I try to help. I try to be actively engaged in offering our views of what we believe can lead to a successful outcome for all parties to the issue.

The same general relationship that holds for the economy—if it does well, we are doing well—also applies to the geopolitical landscape. When the world is more stable, it allows our company to really do the things from a technological, investment, and risk management operating standpoint that make us successful. When the world is unstable, though, it makes it much more difficult for us because we have to operate in a more difficult and uncertain environment. When countries get along and trade policy is positive, we do better. Generally, those are also the same conditions under which the United States tends to thrive.

Though we never forget we are an American company, we operate in many countries around the world. We respect the laws and views of all the countries in which we operate. If it ever gets to a point where we feel we cannot do that in a way that reflects our corporate values, then we probably don't belong in that country any longer. Sometimes it does comes to that point—to a place where we cannot remain in a country because there are too many conflicts with our core principles and views and what we believe to be the best path to success that respects those principles and views. If that path isn't there, there is no reason to stay.

13

I THINK THAT SOMETIMES WHEN PEOPLE MEET ME for the first time they're surprised to find that I'm just a regular guy. There's nothing special about me, but I do my very best every day to reach my potential.

In a perfect world every person would pursue his or her ultimate potential. In a perfect society every person would wake up each morning and want to figure out what he could do that day to move ahead. A person can't do any more than reach his potential—and to the extent that a person "exceeds" his potential all that he is actually exceeding are his own perceptions of what he was capable of. While no person can do more than reach his potential, it is certainly possible for a person to not reach it. That is an unfortunate circumstance. In fact, when that happens it is not healthy for society. You don't have to be president of the United States or the chairman and CEO of a big corporation to reach your potential; you might not ever be a manager or supervisor. It doesn't matter what your title or job is—what matters is how you do your job. I worked as a janitor when I was a teenager, and I just wanted to be the best janitor I could be. I did the work that was required of me as well as I could. I had no idea what the future would bring, but while I was a janitor I gave it my all.

I think that our society would be quite different if every person did everything he could to work toward his potential. That includes working to improve his own life, and the lives of his family and friends, church, school, and community. Everyone would enjoy a better life, and that life would always be on a path of permanent improvement. We live in a productive society, but I think people often shirk their responsibility to contribute to society. If the number of people committed to actively giving back to society shrinks to a small enough number, we will quickly find ourselves in an untenable situation. No society can grow and prosper if its people only look to their own wants and needs.

I also believe that it is crucial that we don't take ourselves too seriously. A good sense of humor is important for balance in both our personal and work lives. It's important when you are working with a group of people on a project, for example, that there be enough levity present that the weight of expectations for the work you are doing doesn't stifle your efforts. Humor can keep your team engaged and nimble, which means they will be efficient.

Another thing that can help you to remain efficient is to keep focused on what is in front of you at the moment, and not spend any time worrying about anything extraneous. I try to focus on the things that I have control of, and not get too caught up in the things that I don't have control of. I try to influence the things I think I can influence, where I think I can make a difference. That is what is within my power to do.

I am engaged in trying to help build a society in which my grandchildren can thrive. Because of my position I have had the privilege of having personal access to just about anyone. I have been able to express my views on a wide range of topics to people that are positioned to make choices that can have a big impact on many others. To be sure, not all of my ideas are accepted. That's fine. At least I know I have done what I can. Getting turned down now and then doesn't mean I will ever give up on what I believe.

A lot of things are happening in the world today that I think are extremely positive and bode well for the future. At the same time, there are also plenty of signs that seem to suggest that our country is very near a tipping point. That's all the more reason for me to do everything I can to ensure that the direction we head as a society and as a nation is a positive one. I'm going to keep at it.

I might have to adjust my tactics over time. Today, I try to impact situations head on. I get my share of criticism when I do, but that's beside the point. If, for no other reason than the position I have held, people are interested in hearing what I have to say. That has been quite a responsibility. I do my best to be consistent, including the mindset I take into my work. I have found that even when I am deeply worried about an issue, I can never perform at my best if I am operating from a negative perspective. I simply cannot be in a pessimistic place and produce my best work. I am at my best when I am optimistic. My wife has accused me of being a Pollyanna. That's not really correct because to be a Pollyanna you can't be realistic, and if I didn't think my views were realistic, I would not share them. To be optimistic is to recognize that there *is* a way forward. So long as I can see a way forward, I will have something to say about how we can best pursue it. I will keep preaching until nobody will listen to me. That will happen at some point, but that day isn't here as I write these words. When it does come I will just have to figure out how to influence people when nobody wants to listen.

"Just do the best job you can do," my mother has always said. That guiding principle has applied in my career and everywhere else in my life, too. Doing your best does not mean you won't make mistakes; I have made plenty, and I will make more. Doing your best also does not mean that everything will always work out the way you want. That is to be expected. The truth is that if you are not experiencing some disappointments or failures, you are probably not working hard enough at it.

I am comfortable with that knowledge and comfortable in the role I have been able to play in a great organization filled with remarkable people. Along the way I have had tremendous support from the people that have worked for me, and beside me. I have been blessed with a team of smart, dedicated people for whom I have enormous respect. It has been a privilege to be around them day in and day out. It is also one of the reasons I have never worried much about the details; my policy has been to let people do what they're good at, knowing that when they do, everything will be just fine.

I have always tried to listen to and think about different points of view as a way of making the most informed decisions possible. Other times I know that I just need to trust my own instincts. I try not to get too caught up in knowing the difference between the two approaches, either. Tomorrow will come, and there will be another chance to do something even better. That's life—it's what you get up and do. I don't get up in the morning and immediately think about what's blocking my way or about something that might have gone less than perfect. I get up and think about what has to get done today.

That's all I can do. In the grand scheme of things, I am one man. I am not very important. I have never believed that it was all about me or that I was bigger in any way than the people around me. I am not. I do believe that I am here for a reason and that it will all play out the right way if I do the right things and take care of what is in front of me.

A few years after I retire, nobody will remember who I was. That is perfectly okay with me.

I have lived a privileged life. God has given me some wonderful things to do, and I know He's not done with me yet. I will just keep plugging away.

Editor's Note

On February 1, 2017, Rex Wayne Tillerson was sworn in as the 69th United States Secretary of State.